YORK NOTES

A MIDSUMMER NIGHT'S DREAM

WILLIAM SHAKESPEARE

Notes by Michael Sherborne

Longman
is an imprint of

PEARSON

YORK
PRESS

The right of Michael Sherborne to be identified as the Author of this Work has been asserted by him in accordance with the Copyright, Designs and Patents Act 1988

YORK PRESS
322 Old Brompton Road, London SW5 9JH

PEARSON EDUCATION LIMITED
Edinburgh Gate, Harlow,
Essex CM20 2JE, United Kingdom

Associated companies, branches and representatives throughout the world

First published 2000

This new and fully revised edition 2013

10 9 8 7 6 5 4 3 2 1

ISBN 978–1–4479–4884–1

Illustration on page 9 by Neil Gower

Phototypeset by Carnegie Book Production

Printed in Italy

Photo credits: © INTERFOTO/Alamy for page 6/© Alisa Andrews / Alamy for page 7 / picsbyst/Shutterstock.com for page 10 / isak55/ Shutterstock.com for page 11 / yurikov/Shutterstock.com for page 12 / iodrakon/Shutterstock.com for page 13 / Purestock/Getty Images for page 14 / Mel Curtis/Getty Images for page 15 / Marketa Ebert/Getty Images for page 16 / Katrina Brown/Shutterstock.com for page 17 / ©iStockphoto.com/amanitephoto for page 18 / White Room/Shutterstock.com for page 19 / Paula Connelly/Getty Images for page 20 / scphoto60/Shutterstock.com for page 21 / Wollertz/Shutterstock.com for page 22 / ©iStockphoto.com/fotogaby for page 23 / Vinnikava Viktoryia/Shutterstock.com for page 24 / ©iStockphoto.com/pokosuke for page 25 / ©iStockphoto.com/stada for page 26 / Suppakij1017/Shutterstock.com for page 27 / ©iStockphoto.com/WLDavies for page 28 / Vladitto/Shutterstock.com for page 29 / ©iStockphoto.com/ioseph for page 30 / ©iStockphoto.com/redhumv for page 31 top / Maxim Khytra/Shutterstock.com for page 31 bottom / White Room/Shutterstock.com for page 32 / solarseven/Shutterstock.com for page 33 top / iko/Shutterstock.com for page 33 bottom / Peshkova/Shutterstock.com for page 34 / Photoasket/Shutterstock.com for page 35 / © Gaertner/Alamy for page 37 / MaXx Images/Getty Images for page 38 / Artem Mazunov/Shutterstock.com for page 39 / Vadim Georgiev/Shutterstock.com for page 40 / esthAlto/Sanna Lindberg/Getty Images for page 41/ Cavan Images/Getty Images for page 42 / iodrakon/Shutterstock.com for page 43 / AXL/Shutterstock.com for page 44 / ©iStockphoto.com/Paula Connelly for page 45 / ©iStockphoto.com/ioseph for page 46 / SasPartout/Shutterstock.com for page 46 bottom / ollyy/Shutterstock.com for page 47 / ©iStockphoto.com/SensorSpot for page 48 / Paolo Sa/Shutterstock.com for page 49 / © Copyright Bryan Alldredge, All Rights Reserved/Getty Images for page 50 / ©iStockphoto. com/Zhenikeyev for page 51 / Oleg Gekman/Shutterstock.com for page 52 / White Room/Shutterstock.com for page 53 / Photosani/ Shutterstock.com for page 54 / Tischenko Irina/Shutterstock.com for page 55 / Natalia Klenova/Shutterstock.com for page 56 / mffoto/ Shutterstock.com for page 57 / Mayer George/Shutterstock.com for page 58 / iofoto/Shutterstock.com for page 59 top / Justin Black/ Shutterstock.com for page 59 bottom / Christoph Weihs/Shutterstock.com for page 60 top / Aleksandar Mijatovic/Shutterstock.com for page 60 bottom / StandOd/Shutterstock.com for page 61 / Anest/Shutterstock.com for page 62 / Lance Bellers/Shutterstock.com for page 63 top / Kamira/Shutterstock.com for page 63 bottom / V. J. Matthew/Shutterstock.com for page 64 / Karlosk/Shutterstock.com for page 65 / Sergey_Bogomyako/Shutterstock.com for page 66 / Snvv/Shutterstock.com for page 67 middle / RTimages/Shutterstock. com for page 67 bottom / Michelangelus/Shutterstock.com for page 68 / MJHT/Shutterstock.com for page 69 top / © Shawn Van Daele/ Getty Images for page 69 bottom / Danita Delimont/Getty Images for page 70 / ©iStockphoto.com/stocknshares for page 71 / © Travel Pictures/Alamy for page 72 / ©iStockphoto.com/msymons for page 73 top / © Classic Image/Alamy for page 73 bottom / Garsya/ Shutterstock.com for page 74 top/ Daniilantiq/Shutterstock.com for page 74 bottom / ©iStockphoto.com/whitemay for page 75 / anyaivanova/Shutterstock.com for page 76 middle / pjhpix/Shutterstock.com for page 76 bottom / © Pictorial Press Ltd/Alamy for page 77 top / © AF archive/Alamy for page 77 bottom / olivier/Shutterstock.com for page 78 top / Africa Studio/Shutterstock.com for page 78 bottom / kuppa/Shutterstock.com for page 79 / ©iStockphoto.com/Goldfaery for page 93 / ©iStockphoto.com/skynesher for page 95

CONTENTS

PART FOUR: STRUCTURE, FORM AND LANGUAGE

PART FIVE: CONTEXTS AND CRITICAL DEBATES

PART SIX: GRADE BOOSTER

ESSENTIAL STUDY TOOLS

PART ONE: INTRODUCING *A MIDSUMMER NIGHT'S DREAM*

HOW TO STUDY *A MIDSUMMER NIGHT'S DREAM*

READING THE PLAY

Read the play once, fairly quickly, for pleasure. This will give you a good sense of the over-arching shape of the plot, and a good feel for the highs and lows of the action, the pace and style, and the sequence in which information is withheld or revealed. You could ask yourself:

- How do individual characters change or develop? How do my own responses to them change?
- How does Shakespeare allow the audience to see into the minds and motives of the characters? Does he use asides, **soliloquies** or other dramatic devices, for example?
- What sort of language do different characters use? Does Shakespeare use **imagery**, or recurring **motifs** or **symbols**?
- Are the events presented chronologically, or is the time scheme altered in some way?
- What impressions do the locations and settings, such as the forest, make on my reading and response to the play?
- How could the play be presented on the stage in different ways? How could different types of performance affect the audience's interpretation of the play?

On your second reading, make detailed notes around the key areas highlighted above and in the Assessment Objectives, such as form, language, structure (AO2), links and connections to other texts (AO3) and the context/background for the play (AO4). These may seem quite demanding, but these Notes will suggest particular elements to explore or jot down.

INTERPRETING OR CRITIQUING THE PLAY

Although it's not helpful to think in terms of the play being 'good' or 'bad', you should consider the different ways the play can be read. How have critics responded to it? Do their views match yours – or do you take a different viewpoint? Are there different ways you can interpret specific events, characters or settings? This is a key aspect in AO3, and it can be helpful to keep a log of your responses and the various perspectives, which are expressed both by established critics, but also by classmates, your teacher, or other readers.

REFERENCES AND SOURCES

You will be expected to draw on critics' or reviewers' comments, and refer to relevant literary or historical sources that might have influenced Shakespeare or his contemporaries. Make sure you make accurate, clear notes of writers or sources you have used, for example noting down titles of works, authors' names, website addresses, dates, etc. You may not have to reference all these things when you respond to a text, but knowing the source of your information will allow you to go back to it, if need be – and to check its accuracy and relevance.

REVISING FOR AND RESPONDING TO AN ASSESSED TASK OR EXAM QUESTION

The structure and the contents of these Notes are designed to help to give you the relevant information or ideas you need to answer tasks you have been set. First, work out the key words or ideas from the task (for example, 'form', 'Act I', 'Titania', etc.), then read the relevant parts of the Notes that relate to these terms or words, selecting what is useful for revision or written response. Then, turn to **Part Six: Grade Booster** for help in formulating your actual response.

GRADE BOOSTER `A02`

Finding good quotations to support your interpretation of the characters will greatly enhance and strengthen your points.

CHECK THE BOOK `A01`

The York Handbook *Dictionary of Literary Terms*, by Martin Gray, provides explanations of the special vocabulary that will help you understand and write about plays like *A Midsummer Night's Dream*.

A MIDSUMMER NIGHT'S DREAM IN CONTEXT

WILLIAM SHAKESPEARE'S LIFE AND TIMES

1564	William Shakespeare born into a well-to-do family in Stratford-upon-Avon, the eldest son and third child of eight
1566	William Adlington's translation of Apuleius's *Golden Ass*
1567	Arthur Golding's translation of Ovid's *Metamorphoses*
1579	Sir Thomas North's translation of Plutarch's *Life of Theseus*
1582	Shakespeare marries Anne Hathaway when he is eighteen and she is twenty-six. They have three children: Susanna (b. 1583), and twins Judith and Hamnet (b. 1585; Hamnet d. 1596)
Early 1590s	Shakespeare moves to London and establishes himself as an actor and playwright
1594–5	*A Midsummer Night's Dream* is written and performed
1600	*A Midsummer Night's Dream* printed (the First Quarto)
1616	Shakespeare dies at the age of 52 after retiring to Stratford in 1611
1623	First collected volume of Shakespeare's plays published (the First Folio)

CONTEXT **A04**

A Midsummer Night's Dream was first printed in 1600 (the First Quarto), then reprinted with minor alterations in 1619 (the Second Quarto). In 1623 the play was included in a collected edition of Shakespeare's works (the First Folio). The Folio text was based on the Second Quarto, but it corrected some earlier mistakes and also gave indications of how the play was staged. Modern editions of the play are based on the First Quarto, but also incorporate some material from the First Folio.

SHAKESPEARE'S DRAMATIC CAREER

Between the late 1580s and 1613, Shakespeare wrote thirty-seven plays, and contributed to some by other dramatists. He began in the late 1580s and early 1590s by rewriting earlier plays and working with plotlines inspired by the Classics. He concentrated on **comedies** (such as *The Comedy of Errors*, 1590–4, which derived from the Latin playwright Plautus), and plays dealing with English history, though he also tried his hand at bloodthirsty revenge **tragedy** (*Titus Andronicus*, 1592–3, indebted to both Ovid and Seneca). During the 1590s Shakespeare developed his expertise in these kinds of plays to write comic masterpieces such as *A Midsummer Night's Dream* (1594–5) and *As You Like It* (1599–1600), together with history plays such as *Henry IV* (1596–8) and *Henry V* (1598–9).

As the new century began, he produced an extraordinary sequence of tragic masterpieces: *Hamlet* (1600–1), *Othello* (1602–4), *King Lear* (1605–6), *Macbeth* (1605–6) and *Antony and Cleopatra* (1606). In the last years of his dramatic career, Shakespeare wrote a group of plays of a quite different kind: 'romances' like *The Winter's Tale* and *The Tempest* (both 1610–11) which reprise many of the situations and **themes** of the earlier dramas but in fantastical and exotic forms involving music, mime, dance and tableaux, having something of the qualities of masques and pageants. *The Tempest* features a male authority figure who deceives others magically, assisted by a spirit, and it explores themes of theatricality and love, so recalling *A Midsummer Night's Dream*.

SHAKESPEARE AND THE WRITING OF A MIDSUMMER NIGHT'S DREAM

A Midsummer Night's Dream cannot be dated precisely, but must have been performed by 1598 because in that year it was mentioned by the writer Francis Meres. It is unlikely that it had been written before 1594, the year of Prince Henry's baptism at the Scottish court, when a plan to employ a lion in the celebrations had to be abandoned on grounds of safety, since this incident probably suggested Snout's anxious query, 'Will not the ladies be afeard of the lion?' (III.1.21). The attempts of scholars to find further topical references in the play have proved indecisive. Taking into account stylistic features, such as rhyme, **imagery** and **rhetorical figures**, most people have agreed that the play originated in the period 1594–5, perhaps with minor revisions later. *Romeo and Juliet* is usually dated at around the same time, and the resemblance between the suicides of those two young lovers and the story of Pyramus and Thisbe suggests that the comedy and the tragedy are intended to some degree to make up a pair.

Unlike most of Shakespeare's plays, *A Midsummer Night's Dream* seems to have been written using original material. It is also unusual in combining three stories, introduced one after another, then woven into an elaborate unity: the story of two pairs of lovers who defy parental disapproval, break up, make up and finally marry; the story of a group of amateur actors, preparing a performance for a wedding celebration, whose blundering efforts **parody** the whole business of putting on a play; finally, the story of a quarrel among a band of fairies, who secretly observe and influence the actions of the others. While the stories may be original, Shakespeare still drew many ideas from his reading, especially from Ovid's *Metamorphoses*, Chaucer's *Knight's Tale* and Apuleius's *Golden Ass* (see **Part Five: Literary background**).

SHAKESPEARE'S THEATRE

Attending the theatre in Shakespeare's time was very different from today. Performances took place in the daytime and in the open air. Wealthier spectators sat in covered galleries, while 'groundlings' stood and watched for a penny. Audiences were less polite than today. Some came in late, interrupted or even got on to the stage. The stage itself was partially covered by a canopy. On either side at the back was a door. These led into the dressing room (the 'tiring house', mentioned by Peter Quince in III.1.4) and it was by means of these doors that actors entered and left the stage. In Act II Scene 1 Oberon and Titania use them to enter from opposite sides and confront one another centre stage. Between the doors was a small recess or alcove which was curtained off. Such a 'discovery place' would have served for Titania's bower in Act II Scene 2 and Act III Scene 1.

Theatrical conventions were very different from today. All the female roles were played by boys. Plays were preceded and followed by jigs and clowning, like the bergomask dance at the end of *A Midsummer Night's Dream*, and the pace of the drama was much faster than we are used to. Exits and entrances were written in as part of the script: characters speak as they enter or leave the stage in order to avoid creating an awkward silence while they take up their positions. There were no intervals between acts, and very little in the way of props or scenery, which is why characters often tell us where they are, as Quince does at the start of Act III Scene 1.

SETTING

A Midsummer Night's Dream is set in ancient Athens, but with little attempt at historical accuracy. In many respects the play sounds as if it is set in Elizabethan England. Theseus may be a character from ancient myth, but he is called a Duke and behaves like an English aristocrat. References to a natural world of cuckoos, choughs and violets, and a social world of Saint Valentine's day, Maying and the board game nine men's morris, create a sense of English country life. The fairies, despite their world travels, come straight from English folklore, as Oberon confirms by his reference to Queen Elizabeth I (II.1.163). The craftsmen, similarly, speak in English idioms and perform a play which is English in style.

However, there are several reasons why the choice of ancient Athens as a setting is a good one. It takes the audience into a world which is distinct from their own, where fantastic events do not seem so jarringly unbelievable. Once we have imagined that we are in the time of Theseus, it is no big step to imagine mischievous spirits and magic spells. We also find ourselves in a world before Christianity, so it is possible to introduce fairies and show humans controlled by spirits without causing offence. The play does not look as if it is questioning or mocking religion, only having fun at the expense of the ancient past.

Moreover, Athens is a famous city in the history of philosophy, known for its great thinkers, Socrates, Plato and Aristotle. This reputation enhances the contrast between the rational daylight world of Athens and the night-time world of the wood outside. The wood (a word which in Elizabethan English could also mean 'mad') is a place of dreams and imagination, where the mortal characters blunder uncertainly in the dark and are beset by nasty surprises and miraculous joys. Shakespeare does not spoil the effect by spelling out that the wood represents the mysteries of love, which perplex the four lovers, and of art, which overwhelm the craftsmen, though he does seem to indicate it later through Theseus's comment that 'The lunatic, the lover and the poet / Are of imagination all compact' (V.1.7–8).

STUDY FOCUS: KEY ISSUES A03

LOVE

Much fun is extracted from the irrationality of love. The fairies' magic juice speeds up the process of falling in and out of love, turning painful emotions and personal conflicts into knockabout farce. Yet the importance and dangers of this powerful emotion remain clear.

MARRIAGE

The play is full of transformations. The most important celebrate growth (from youth to maturity, singleness to marriage) or reconcile opposites (day and night, male and female, reason and imagination). Three couples get married at the end of the play, but the marriage of opposites is a **theme** underlying the whole comedy.

GENDER

Theseus has defeated Hippolyta in battle. Oberon tricks and degrades Titania with his magic. Does the play then firmly reflect the gender assumptions of its time, or are there elements of the play which question these, showing a sympathy for the female characters which connects with a modern audience?

THEATRE

The antics of the craftsmen as they rehearse and perform 'Pyramus and Thisbe' constantly draws our attention to how drama works. This risks undermining our belief in the play as a whole, but Shakespeare has enough confidence in his writing and his actors to trust that it will have a different effect. Instead, he is encouraging us to see links between play-acting and life outside the theatre, where we are at the mercy of hidden influences and play many roles. From this perspective the hero of the drama may well be Bottom, who, for all his deficiencies, has the natural wisdom to accept any role in which he finds himself and the positive spirit to see it through in style.

GRADE BOOSTER A02

To show your understanding of structure for AO2, consider how a scene reflects the events of other scenes around it. In the night scenes, in particular, how do the lovers behave differently from their daytime selves, how might Oberon and Titania relate to Theseus and Hippolyta, how does Bottom as Titania's temporary partner contrast with Oberon?

CHARACTERS IN *A MIDSUMMER NIGHT'S DREAM*

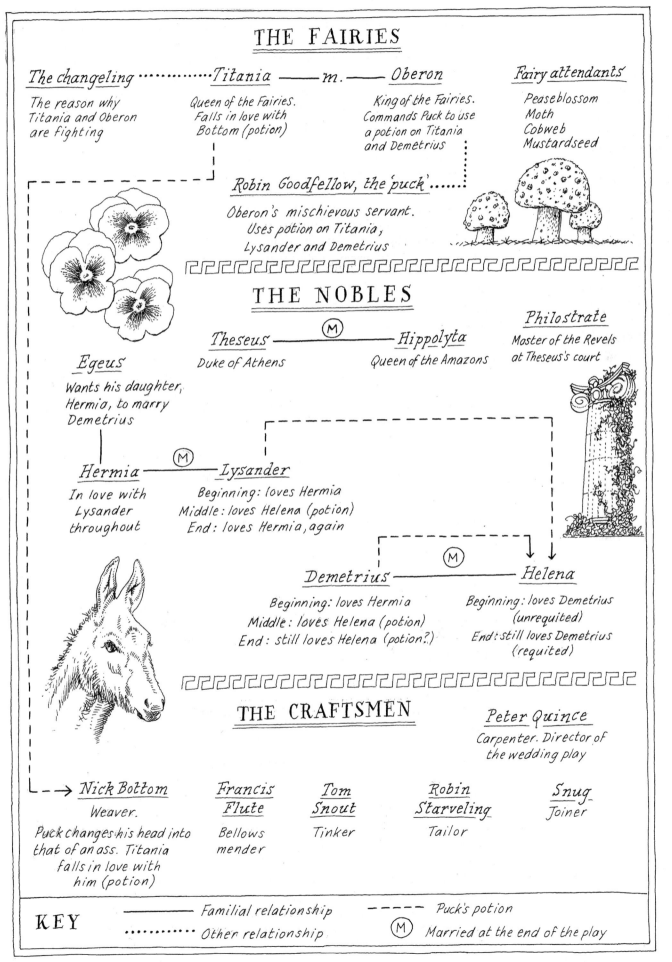

THE FAIRIES

The changeling
The reason why Titania and Oberon are fighting

Titania —— m. —— **Oberon**

Titania
Queen of the Fairies. Falls in love with Bottom (potion)

Oberon
King of the Fairies. Commands Puck to use a potion on Titania and Demetrius

Fairy attendants
Peaseblossom
Moth
Cobweb
Mustardseed

Robin Goodfellow, the 'puck'
Oberon's mischievous servant. Uses potion on Titania, Lysander and Demetrius

THE NOBLES

Theseus —— Ⓜ —— **Hippolyta**

Theseus
Duke of Athens

Hippolyta
Queen of the Amazons

Philostrate
Master of the Revels at Theseus's court

Egeus
Wants his daughter, Hermia, to marry Demetrius

Hermia —— Ⓜ —— **Lysander**

Hermia
In love with Lysander throughout

Lysander
Beginning: loves Hermia
Middle: loves Helena (potion)
End: loves Hermia, again

Demetrius —— Ⓜ —— **Helena**

Demetrius
Beginning: loves Hermia
Middle: loves Helena (potion)
End: still loves Helena (potion?)

Helena
Beginning: loves Demetrius (unrequited)
End: still loves Demetrius (requited)

THE CRAFTSMEN

Peter Quince
Carpenter. Director of the wedding play

Nick Bottom
Weaver.
Puck changes his head into that of an ass. Titania falls in love with him (potion)

Francis Flute
Bellows mender

Tom Snout
Tinker

Robin Starveling
Tailor

Snug
Joiner

KEY

—— Familial relationship
········· Other relationship
– – – Puck's potion
Ⓜ Married at the end of the play

SYNOPSIS

CONFLICTS OF LOVE

Theseus, Duke of Athens, has conquered Hippolyta, Queen of the Amazons, in battle and is now preparing to marry her. Egeus, an Athenian citizen, comes to him with a complaint that Hermia, his daughter, is refusing to marry Demetrius, the husband he has chosen for her. She instead loves a rival suitor, Lysander. Egeus demands that she do as he orders or be put to death. Theseus offers her a third option, that of becoming a nun. Hermia refuses to change her mind, however, and Lysander casts doubt on Demetrius's suitability as a husband by pointing out that he had previously been in love with another young woman called Helena. While Theseus takes Egeus and Demetrius off to give them some private advice, Lysander persuades Hermia to elope with him. They decide to rendezvous in the wood outside Athens that night. They then reveal their plan to Helena, but she is so besotted with Demetrius that she betrays their secret in order to have an excuse to see him. Demetrius decides to pursue the couple, Helena to follow him.

CONTEXT | **A04**

In Shakespeare's London there were between five and eight theatres open at any one time. Audience figures were very large, with 18,000 to 24,000 people visiting the theatre each week.

IN THE WOOD

The four lovers are not alone in the wood. Some Athenian craftsmen, who want to put on a play for the duke's wedding celebrations, have decided to rehearse there that night. The leader of the group is Peter Quince, a carpenter, but their efforts are generally dominated by the exuberant personality of a weaver named Nick Bottom. The craftsmen lack both experience in the art of drama and talent, but are enthusiastically determined to stage their play nonetheless. Oberon and Titania, the king and queen of the fairies, also meet in the wood, each accompanied by their followers. They have fallen out with each other over possession of a human boy, a conflict which has upset the balance of nature, causing severe weather problems for human beings. Titania is caring for the boy and refuses to hand him over to Oberon. The meeting between them leads only to further quarrelling.

MAGIC SPELLS

Oberon sends his helper, Robin Goodfellow, a puck or goblin, to fetch some magic juice with which to punish Titania. Oberon puts the juice on her eyes while she is asleep, knowing that it will make her fall in love with the next creature she sees. While travelling through the wood, Oberon has observed Demetrius spurning Helena and, thinking to help the young woman, he tells Robin to apply the juice to Demetrius's eyes also. Instead, Robin finds Lysander sleeping, mistakes him for Demetrius and applies the juice to him. When Lysander awakens, he immediately falls in love with the passing Helena and abandons Hermia. Robin, meanwhile, sees the craftsmen rehearsing their play and decides to play a trick on them. He uses magic to give Nick Bottom the head of an ass. After the others have fled in terror at this transformation, Titania awakens and, under the spell of the juice, falls in love with Bottom.

CONFUSION AND HARMONY

Seeing Demetrius quarrelling with Hermia, who continues to reject him, Oberon realises that Robin's intervention must have misfired. Trying to put the situation right, he applies the juice to Demetrius's eyes when Helena is nearby, but the immediate outcome of this is that Demetrius and Lysander, both of whom have previously been in love with Hermia, are now in love with Helena. She, however, believes that they are mocking and tormenting her, probably with the connivance of Hermia who, joining the others at this point, is baffled to be rejected and insulted by her Lysander. To prevent violence between the lovers, Oberon orders Robin to intervene again, drawing them apart. Once they have grown weary and fallen asleep, Robin puts an antidote juice on Lysander's eyes to take away his love for Helena. Oberon and Robin then remove the magic spells from Titania (who has in the meantime agreed to hand over the boy) and from Bottom. The king and queen of the fairies are reunited.

HAPPY ENDINGS

Theseus and his companions, out early in the morning, discover the four lovers lying asleep in the wood and awaken them. The four explain, in so far as they are able to, their changed feelings. Theseus overrules the objections of Egeus and declares that the two couples shall be married alongside him and Hippolyta. When everyone else has left the wood, Bottom awakens, reflects on his strange 'dream', then hurries to find the other craftsmen. They are lamenting Bottom's loss and the consequent cancellation of their play when he arrives to announce that all is well.

CELEBRATION

On the evening of the three marriages, Theseus agrees to the staging of the craftsmen's play, a **tragedy** called 'Pyramus and Thisbe'. The play is badly written and acted, but in practice its defects make it hugely entertaining and Bottom triumphs in the leading role. When all the humans have gone to bed, the fairies enter the house. They bless those who reside there and their children to come.

> **CONTEXT** **A02**
>
> *A Midsummer Night's Dream* is one of Shakespeare's most popular stories, constantly staged, frequently filmed, and still being used as the basis for new stories such as *This Must be Love* by Tui Sutherland and *Eastwords* by Kalyan Ray (both 2004).

ACT I SCENE 1

SUMMARY

- Duke Theseus is looking forward to marrying Hippolyta, the Queen of the Amazons.
- Egeus arrives with his daughter Hermia and her two suitors, Lysander and Demetrius. Hermia is in love with Lysander, but Egeus insists that she must marry Demetrius or be executed.
- While Theseus offers Egeus and Demetrius some advice in private, Lysander persuades Hermia to run away with him.
- They confide their plan to Helena, but she is so infatuated with Demetrius that she decides to tell him about the plan in order to have an excuse to see him.

ANALYSIS

A COMEDY OF LOVE

CONTEXT **A04**

Hippolyta was the Queen of the Amazons, a legendary nation of female warriors. She and Theseus later had a son called Hippolytus. *A Midsummer Night's Dream* begins shortly before the couple's wedding.

The emphasis on marriage and happiness in the opening conversation prepares us for a **comedy**. Theseus sets the tone of the play by comparing the moon to a widow spending her husband's money to the annoyance of her son, who is eager to inherit it. Starting with this speech, the play sets out to expose the uncomfortable nature of human motives but in a humorous spirit, not a bitter one.

The word 'moon' is used three times in the first two speeches and the moon is mentioned seven times in the scene as a whole, establishing it as a key **image** in the play. The moon's associations with madness and change make it an appropriate accompaniment to a comedy of love. (See the section on **Imagery and symbolism** in **Part Four: Language**.)

Theseus fought Hippolyta but now he loves her. This change of attitude introduces the **theme** that love is irrational and powerful. We also see that love may not be straightforward or positive in its effects, for it is not clear whether Hippolyta is as happy to be getting married to Theseus as he is to be marrying her. She says little in this scene and what she does say is surprisingly unrevealing of her emotions. In some productions she is played as a loving bride, but in others she is seems to be going through the ceremony reluctantly as part of a peace treaty.

STUDY FOCUS: THE MARRIAGE OF OPPOSITES A02

Theseus and Hippolyta express contrasting attitudes. He is impatient for the wedding night and expresses his frustrations in a joking fashion; she perceives the time to be going quickly and speaks in a quieter, more elevated tone. They even see the moon in opposed ways. He speaks of the moon as waning and compares it to an old woman, she looks ahead to the new moon and compares it to a bow ready to be fired. However, in a play which is constantly bringing together opposites (such as day and night, city and wood, upper and lower class, and mortals and fairies), we should not assume that their contrasting states of mind will necessarily end in conflict. Instead they might turn out to be complementary.

CONTEXT A04

Egeus wants to impose a forced marriage on his daughter, Hermia. He claims he has the right to do so under Greek law ('the ancient privilege of Athens', line 41). In Shakespeare's England, marriages arranged by parents were quite common among wealthy families, but forced marriages like this one were rare and widely condemned.

THE THREAT OF EGEUS

Egeus, whose intervention introduces the **plot** of the young lovers, is a typical figure of comedy, the angry father who obstructs true love. His emphasis on the words 'me', 'my' and 'mine' (lines 23–42) show his self-centred nature. His accusing tone, repetitive complaints and unreasonable demands ensure we have little sympathy or respect for him. Theseus feels obliged to support Egeus's rights as a father, but he speaks gently to Hermia, gives her four days to reach a final decision and allows her the further option of becoming a nun. In keeping with his own desire for the 'nuptial hour' (line 1) and the focus of the play on marriage, he does not make the celibate life sound attractive (the words 'shady … barren … faint … cold … fruitless' and 'thorn', lines 71–7, are not inviting). When Theseus takes Egeus and Demetrius off for some 'private schooling' (line 116), we can reasonably assume that he will be critical of their attitude to Hermia, even though he feels obliged to stand up for the men in public.

His remark to Hippolyta ('What cheer, my love?', line 122) suggests that she looks unhappy with the situation. Does she perhaps see in Hermia's plight a reflection of her own?

ONLY A GIRL?

Hermia's life is controlled by men whom she has to obey. Theseus even explains to Hermia that, as her father has created her, she should think of him as a 'god' who can do what he likes with her (lines 147–51). Perhaps this is only what we should expect from someone who has recently defeated a nation of independent women, the Amazons. Today we would describe such assumptions as patriarchal and unfair. But does the play support them? Egeus has little resemblance to a god, Theseus has no intention of sentencing Hermia to death and, as the story develops, we are expected to follow sympathetically Hermia's attempts to thwart her father. The play is therefore sensitive to gender issues, but it is unlikely to share our modern assumptions about female equality and we need to stay alert to exactly what values it does imply.

GRADE BOOSTER A02

Lysander says Helena not only loves Demetrius but 'dotes, Devoutly dotes, dotes in idolatry' upon him (lines 108–9). The repetition of 'dotes' and of religious language readies us for Helena's comical obsession with Demetrius later in the scene. The claim that he 'made love' to her (line 107) should not be interpreted in the modern sense. It simply means that Demetrius courted Helena.

THE YOUNG LOVERS

The play has begun with two mature lovers looking ahead to their wedding. Now the focus shifts to Hermia and Lysander, who are much younger and whose marriage has been forbidden. They may remind us of Romeo and Juliet, whose story Shakespeare wrote at around the same time as *A Midsummer Night's Dream*. That story ended in **tragedy** and, when Lysander lists ways in which love can come to grief and 'The jaws of darkness do devour it up' (line 148), his tone becomes tragic too. He brightens up when he proposes a plan to meet in the wood and elope, though at this stage of the play we cannot be sure that his ideas for disobedience will have any better outcome than Romeo's.

While we are meant to feel sympathy for Hermia and Lysander, their references to examples of thwarted love from history and mythology reduce our involvement in their feelings. The couple become one example of a common situation. A similar emotional distance is achieved through formal language, such as the balanced **couplets** which, after Helena's arrival, the two young women share ('The more I hate, the more he follows me,' 'The more I love, the more he hateth me', lines 198–9).

Hermia has fond memories of her girlhood friendship with Helena, recalling how they would often lie out in the wood sharing their thoughts (lines 214–6). In contrast, Helena sounds jealous of Hermia, complaining that 'Demetrius loves your fair' (line 182). Love has started to come between these contrasting young women (Hermia is short and dark-haired, Helena tall and blonde), preparing us for the jealousy and rivalry which will erupt in Act III.

BLIND CUPID

When Helena is left alone on the stage, her **soliloquy** referring to Cupid states plainly what will later be shown by the characters' actions, that love is subjective, based on individual feelings, not on reason. Earlier Hermia had wished that her father saw with her eyes (line 56). Helena reintroduces this key **image** of eyes to stress that beauty lies in the eye of the beholder and is therefore liable to be irrational and changeable. Her own misguided decision to tell Demetrius about the elopement reinforces the point, and also leaves us wondering what will happen when she does so.

GLOSSARY

33	**conceits**	fancy articles
45	**Immediately**	at once, with no right of appeal
89	**Diana**	goddess of chastity
171	**Venus' doves**	the doves who were supposed to pull the love goddess's flying chariot
173	**Carthage queen**	Dido, Queen of Carthage, fell in love with Aeneas (the 'false Trojan') and burned herself to death when he left her
191	**translated**	changed
209	**Phoebe**	goddess of the moon

KEY QUOTATIONS: ACT I SCENE 1 **A01**

Key quotation 1:

In her concluding **soliloquy**, Helena reflects that:

'Things base and vile, holding no quantity,
Love can transpose to form and dignity.
Love looks not with the eyes, but with the mind,
And therefore is winged Cupid painted blind.' (lines 232–5)

Possible interpretations:

- Love has the power to confer value on someone who is normally looked down upon.
- Love has the power to make someone fall for an unworthy person or reject someone who might be their ideal partner.
- Even though Helena is able to reflect on the irrationality of love, her understanding of it cannot prevent her from becoming its victim and behaving irrationally too.

CONTEXT **A04**

Helena's views on love draw on the philosophy of Neoplatonism, popular with Renaissance love poets. This maintained that poetic meditation would enable them to refine their desire for physical beauty until it became love of the soul, and finally love for God.

Key quotation 2:

Theseus tells Hermia:

'To you your father should be as a god,
One that composed your beauties; yea, and one
To whom you are but as a form in wax
By him imprinted, and within his power
To leave the figure, or disfigure it.' (lines 47–51)

Possible interpretations:

- Egeus created Hermia and is entitled to do as he wants with her.
- Although Egeus can 'disfigure' her if he wishes, the word implies that Theseus privately thinks it would be an evil thing to do.
- Egeus and Theseus are powerful men conspiring against a young woman who seems defenceless but has no intention of giving in to their intimidating speeches.

Other useful quotations:

Theseus sets the tone of the play: 'Awake the pert and nimble spirit of mirth' (line 14).

Egeus on treating his daughter as a possession: 'As she is mine, I may dispose of her' (line 42).

Hermia on her resistance: 'My soul consents not to give sovereignty' (line 82).

Lysander on the perils of love: 'The course of true love never did run smooth' (line 134).

ACT I SCENE 2

SUMMARY

- Six craftsmen from Athens have decided to stage a play to celebrate the marriage of Theseus and Hippolyta. Peter Quince, the carpenter, takes charge.
- His efforts are disrupted by his leading actor, Nick Bottom, a weaver. Not content with playing the hero, Bottom offers to play all the other parts and regrets that there is no role for a raging tyrant which would allow him to show off his acting at full strength.
- The craftsmen agree to meet for a secret rehearsal that night in the wood.

ANALYSIS

THE COMICAL CRAFTSMEN

The second scene forms a strong contrast to the first, both in content and form. The aristocrats of the first scene speak in **verse**, but the craftsmen speak in **prose**, with less regular rhythm and more **colloquial** expressions. When they do attempt to use a more educated vocabulary, they tend to choose the wrong words and accidentally say something ridiculous. Bottom, for example, confuses 'moderate' with 'aggravate' (line 76), which means entirely the opposite, and 'seemly' (or perhaps 'obscurely') with 'obscenely' (line 100), which has a different meaning altogether. These mistakes are one source of **comedy** in the scene. Another is the craftsmen's naïve assumption that their performance will be so convincing that the audience will not be able to tell the difference between a real lion and Snug the joiner in a costume.

However, most of the comedy comes from the way that Bottom disrupts the meeting, with Quince largely relegated to the role of 'straight man', patiently explaining his plans when he can get a word in, then flattering Bottom out of his sulk. Bottom's behaviour is rather immature, but he is driven by a real enthusiasm for acting and by enjoyment at putting on a show. If he is overbearing, he is also a natural leader, advising and enthusing the others. The audience is expected to laugh at the craftsmen's ignorance, but there is no mistaking their sincerity. Bottom's enthusiasm is difficult to resist.

LAMENTABLE COMEDY

The confusion of **genres** in the title of 'The most lamentable comedy … of Pyramus and Thisbe' (lines 11–12) is laughable. 'Lamentable' means full of sorrow and pity. How can these emotions be appropriate to a comedy? Yet it may be that the mistakes in the craftsmen's title hint at the nature of *A Midsummer Night's Dream* itself. Shakespeare's play is a comedy, but one which contains serious reflection on the human condition and a potentially **tragic** outcome. As events unfold, Lysander and Hermia's attempt to flee from Athens, along with Demetrius's determination to prevent them, could easily lead to the deaths of one or more of the characters.

CONTEXT **A04**

The names of the craftsmen reflect their jobs. Quince the carpenter would use wedges called quines or quoins. Snug the joiner would make snugly tight wooden joints. The name of Flute the bellows-maker suggests a pipe on a bellows-powered church organ, as well as his squeaky voice which has not yet broken. Snout the tinker mends the spouts (or snouts) of kettles. Tailors were often said to be poor and thin, hence the name Starveling. Bottom the weaver unwinds the thread from a bottom or reel.

CONTEXT **A04**

Shakespeare wrote *A Midsummer Night's Dream* for the theatre company to which he belonged, the Lord Chamberlain's Men, and he would have developed many of the characters with specific actors in mind. John Sincklo, who was strikingly thin, must have played Starveling. The role of Bottom would have been taken by the company's star comedian Will Kempe, while Peter Quince would probably have been played by Kempe's 'straight man', Richard Cowley.

STUDY FOCUS: A PLAY ABOUT A PLAY

A02

The craftsmen's preparations for their 'Pyramus and Thisbe' play remind us that we are already watching a play in which the characters are played by actors. The original sixteenth-century audience would have immediately recognised and enjoyed the craftsmen's **parody** of the Elizabethan theatre, with the ranting tyrant's speech and the woman's part played by a man, as well as the actors fussing over their make-up. But might not this reminder spoil the audience's imaginative involvement? Shakespeare must have been very confident in the power of his language and the skill of his actors to survive the challenge. He may also have been keen to establish that this is a play about illusion, role play and imagination, which are important in many aspects of life, not just the theatre. Look out for the way this **theme** is developed as the play progresses.

CONTEXT **A04**

The casting of Flute as Thisbe reminds us that in Shakespeare's day it was unacceptable for women to appear in plays, so the female parts had to be played by men. After Shakespeare, under the religious rule of the Puritans (1642–60), all public theatre was banned. It was only with the restoration of the monarchy in 1660 that actresses finally appeared on the English stage.

CONTEXT **A04**

Saying 'here are your parts' (line 78), Quince gives each man his lines to learn. This was also how Shakespeare's actors worked. As it would be too slow and costly to write out several copies of the play by hand, each actor received only their own lines, together with the words that were their cues to speak. Once they had learned their lines individually, they would meet up to rehearse together before performing the play in public.

WHAT NEXT?

Like the first scene, the second ends with plans to go to the wood, leaving the audience wondering whether the lovers and the craftsmen will meet there and how the two plots might be linked, but feeling sure that, whatever the details, the outcome is bound to be entertaining.

GLOSSARY

22	**Ercles**	Hercules, the great hero of Greek mythology
28	**Phibbus' car**	the chariot of Phoebus Apollo, the sun god
43	**Thisne**	this mysterious word is probably Bottom's attempt at a pet name for Thisbe, though some editors have suggested it means 'in this way'
66–7	**sucking dove**	a confusion between 'sitting dove' and 'sucking lamb'
75–6	**French crowns**	French coins, with a double reference to baldness on the crown of the head caused by the so-called 'French disease', syphilis
79	**con**	learn
88	**hold, or cut bowstrings**	keep to your promise

CHECK THE BOOK   **A04**

Troublesome Things by Diane Purkiss (Penguin, 2000) is a history of fairies which ranges from ancient legend to modern cinema, seeking to explain how and why the appeal of these spirits has changed over time. The book contains an illuminating discussion of *A Midsummer Night's Dream*.

CONTEXT   **A04**

Today people usually imagine fairies as sweet little creatures, but in traditional folklore they were spirits who tormented, bewitched and abducted people, sometimes doing their victims permanent damage. Few of Shakespeare's original audience-members would have believed in fairies, but they would certainly have known various tales about them and would have been intrigued and amused by the doings of the comparatively friendly fairies in this play.

ACT II SCENE 1

SUMMARY

- In the wood an unnamed servant of the fairy queen encounters Robin Goodfellow, a puck or mischievous goblin, who is a servant of the fairy king.
- Robin warns the fairy that Queen Titania and King Oberon have quarrelled and if the two meet there will be a confrontation.
- On arrival, the fairy king and queen accuse one another of romantic attachments to Hippolyta and Theseus. Oberon says they can be friends again if she hands over a young boy to be his chief page.
- Titania declares she will not because of her friendship with the boy's mother who died in childbirth. She and her followers leave.
- Oberon sends Robin to find a magic flower. The juice will make anyone fall in love with the first creature they see and he intends to use it on Titania for his revenge.
- Demetrius comes to the wood to prevent the elopement of Hermia and Lysander. He is followed by the love-struck Helena.
- Oberon sees Demetrius scorn Helena and decides to make him fall in love with her. When Robin brings the flower, Oberon tells the puck to put some juice on the eyes of Demetrius.

ANALYSIS

ENTER THE FAIRIES

We have been introduced to the aristocrats and the craftsmen. This scene brings in a third group of characters, the fairies. With the arrival of Helena and Demetrius towards the end of the scene, the groups begin to come together, making the audience wonder exactly how the three **plots** will interweave. The fairies' speeches turn the wood from the everyday location which it has been so far into a magic world where anything might happen.

For all their power, trickery and quarrelling, and the environmental consequences of their bickering, the fairies are much less threatening than they were often portrayed to be in Elizabethan folklore. Much of the time they seem to be very small – a point established straight away by the fairy's work of placing dew drops in cowslips (lines 14–15), then reinforced soon after by her mention of elves creeping into acorn cups (line 31). Their way of life seems to consist largely of caring for natural objects, dancing and playing pranks. It is a simple, child-like existence, linked to the tradition of **pastoral** poetry by Titania's references to Corin and Phillida (lines 66–8).

After the **iambic pentameter** of the aristocrats and the **prose** of the craftsmen, we experience a further contrast in the **verse** of the fairies, which is more varied in **metre** than the speech of the Athenians. The fairies' speeches readily shift into short, rhyming lines and so become song-like, as in the fairy's first speech. In some productions many of these passages are in fact sung.

THE FAIRIES' NATURE

Shakespeare has to establish the world of the fairies very quickly as there was no settled view among people of his time about what such creatures might be like. He does so through the conversation between Robin and the fairy, sketching their different powers and activities. At the same time, in order to keep the story moving forwards, he firmly signals the coming confrontation between Titania and Oberon.

Like the Roman poet Ovid, whose book *Metamorphoses* was a great influence on *A Midsummer Night's Dream* (see **Part Five: Literary background**), Shakespeare uses his supernatural characters to put forward light-hearted mythical explanations of nature. When, for example, cream fails to turn to butter or someone misses their chair and falls, it is because of an intervention by the puck (lines 34–7 and 52–4).

THE FAIRIES' QUARRELS

The quarrelling of Titania and Oberon makes them a poor advertisement for marriage, to which the other couples in the play look forward to so romantically. The disagreements do not actually dispel their exotic glamour, but are sufficiently out of keeping with it to be amusing. Audiences of Shakespeare's time seem to have had a great fondness for practical jokes – even for ones which to us might seem harsh – so we can assume they would be highly entertained by Robin's mischief-making and the spell which Oberon later casts on Titania. Nonetheless, even they might have had some reservations about the way Titania is treated. Her sympathy for the sufferings of the 'human mortals' (line 101) in the bad weather and floods, and her moving account of her love for her dead 'votress' (line 123), must win some audience sympathy.

CHECK THE FILM A03

The fairies are often acted by a mixture of adults and children. In some productions actors playing humans also play fairies. Ten characters are doubled like this in the 1996 film version (dir. Adrian Noble), including Lindsay Duncan as Hippolyta/Titania and Alex Jennings as Theseus/Oberon. How might pairing characters in this way affect our interpretation of the story?

STUDY FOCUS: LANGUAGE PAINTS PICTURES   A02

Titania's long speech beginning 'These are the forgeries of jealousy' (lines 81–117) is a striking piece of poetry which would be out of place in the mouth of the merely human characters. She creates a vivid impression of the countryside through her series of descriptions, and the way she **personifies** the winds, rivers, seasons and moon suggests her supernatural intimacy with the forces of nature. Titania's appearance may be presented in a variety of ways in the theatre through costumes, make-up and lighting effects, but it is really this speech and the succeeding one about the votress which drive home to the audience that they are not listening to any ordinary character, but to the queen of the fairies. The same may be said of some of Oberon's speeches (for example, the passage beginning 'I know a bank where the wild thyme blows', line 249), although none of his contributions are as sustained so none makes quite so great an impression.

FEMALE FRIENDSHIPS

Titania has given a moving description of the affection between herself and her pregnant votress (lines 123–35). This can be set beside the earlier mention of the girlhood closeness of Hermia and Helena (I.1.213–7). Both friendships are described so as to arouse our imaginative sympathy, but in both cases there seems to be an implication that it is natural for the impact of male concerns to destroy them. Hermia and Helena come into conflict over their boyfriends and now Oberon exerts authority over his wife, claiming he is entitled to take charge of the boy she has adopted and to punish and humiliate her if she challenges his authority. Feminist critics see a pattern running through the play in which we are encouraged to have a degree of sympathy for the women and wish for them to be treated more fairly, but are consistently shown that final authority must belong to men.

STUDY FOCUS: ELIZABETH I

A04

A modern audience is likely to be puzzled by Oberon's remarks about the 'fair vestal' (lines 148–64). The incident is based upon the pageants which were sometimes staged by noblemen at their country houses when the queen came to visit them. In 1575, for example, when Elizabeth I stayed with the Earl of Leicester at Kenilworth, she was treated to a parade on water including a boat in the shape of a dolphin and to a spectacular fireworks display. At a royal entertainment of 1581 the queen watched from a 'Fortress of Perfect Beauty' as courtiers laid siege to her, urging her to surrender to 'virtuous desire'. This was a hint that many of her subjects wanted her to marry and produce an heir, so that the future of the country would be secure. Elizabeth, however, chose to remain a Virgin Queen, and Oberon's words seem to praise this policy. Her chaste nature guards her against the foolish behaviour which love can induce. The point is reinforced shortly afterwards by the behaviour of Helena, whose devotion to Demetrius is so abject that it makes her a laughing stock.

CHECK THE BOOK A03

Shakespeare was not the first to associate Elizabeth I with the fairy world. Fairy pageants had been staged for her entertainment on several occasions. Above all, there was Edmund Spenser's unfinished epic poem *The Faerie Queene*, the first part of which was published in 1590, dedicated to the queen herself. In the complex symbolism of the poem, Gloriana the Fairy Queen stands for Elizabeth, who responded to the compliment by paying Spenser a pension for life.

HELENA AND DEMETRIUS

The arrival of the two mortals brings some lively comedy to the scene. Helena has told Demetrius that he can prevent Hermia and Lysander eloping by intercepting them in the wood, but he has not yet managed to find them. Both his exasperation and his desperation to escape from Helena are amusing. Helena's shameless pursuit of the reluctant Demetrius is even more so. As she says herself, 'We should be wooed, and were not made to woo' (line 242). Feminists may be uncomfortable that the humour here comes from female humiliation, but Helena's grovelling invitation to be treated like a dog, so long as she is allowed to follow Demetrius (lines 203–10), and his desperate attempts to run away from her (line 227) are a guaranteed source of laughter for any audience.

GLOSSARY

7	**moon's sphere**	the moon, planets and stars were thought to be fixed to transparent spheres which rotated about the Earth
10	**pensioners**	royal guard
54	**'Tailor'**	the expression probably refers to someone falling on their backside or 'tail'
66–8	**Corin and Phillida**	names traditionally used for shepherds and shepherdesses in **pastoral** poetry

GLOSSARY (continued)

69	**step** the furthest limit of exploration	
78–80	**Perigenia ... Aegles ... Ariadne ... Antiopa** lovers of Theseus during his legendary adventures	
92	**continents** banks	
98	**nine-men's-morris** a game with pegs, which could be played outdoors by cutting a pattern of squares in the turf	
109	**Hiems** winter **personified** as an old man	
123	**votress** a woman who has taken vows	
168	**love-in-idleness** pansy	
192	**wood** maddened	
220	**Your virtue is my privilege** your good qualities are my guarantee of safety	
231	**Apollo ... and Daphne** in the legend, the god Apollo chased the nymph Daphne. She was able to escape his lust only by being turned into a laurel tree	
256	**Weed** garment	

KEY QUOTATIONS: ACT II SCENE 1   (A01)

Key quotation 1:

Hippolyta claims that the recent extreme weather conditions have been caused by their quarrel, 'We are their parents and original' (line 117).

Possible interpretations:

- The fairies are nature spirits whose job it is to keep the ecology in order.
- Serious family quarrels of the kind we see in the play tend to spread trouble to those all around them.
- There is a divine order built into the universe which everyone should respect.

Key quotation 2:

Helena complains to Demetrius, 'You draw me, you hard-hearted adamant!' (line 195).

Possible interpretations:

- He attracts her as powerfully as a magnet attracts iron.
- His lack of affection for her shows that his heart is as hard as rock.
- Helena has no control over her feelings for Demetrius and she is unwilling to accept responsibility for her actions.

Other useful quotations:

The puck: 'I am that merry wanderer of the night' (line 43).

Demetrius's feelings about his situation: 'wood [madness] within this wood' (line 192).

Helena's submissiveness: 'I am your spaniel' (line 203).

Helena's discomfort: 'We should be wooed, and were not made to woo.' (line 242).

GRADE BOOSTER   (A02)

Remember that *A Midsummer Night's Dream* is a play, not a novel. When discussing the significance of a quotation, try to consider how the actor might have spoken the lines and their behaviour as they did so. In this scene, for example, does Demetrius speak to Helena in a fierce, bullying way or is he weakly desperate to escape from her, or does his performance include both these attitudes?

ACT II SCENE 2

SUMMARY

- Oberon puts the magic juice on the eyes of the sleeping Titania.
- Lysander and Hermia, lost in the wood, decide to stop and sleep. The puck finds them and mistakenly puts the juice on Lysander's eyes, thinking he is Demetrius.
- Lysander awakens and under the influence of the juice falls in love with Helena. She thinks that he is only mocking her and goes off feeling insulted. He pursues her, abandoning the sleeping Hermia.
- Hermia awakens from a nightmare that she is being attacked by a snake and is shocked to find Lysander missing. She goes in search of him.

ANALYSIS

THE MAGIC JUICE

The opening of the scene, with Titania issuing orders to the fairies before being sung to sleep, creates a world of pure enchantment, but it is not long before it is disrupted by the arrival of Oberon with the magic juice. His anointing of Titania's eyes and his final malicious wish ('Wake when some vile thing is near', line 40) make us anxious to see what will happen when she wakes up. Whatever else occurs in the meantime, we never quite forget that Titania is sleeping close by. In the original production she would probably have been placed in a curtained recess at the back of the stage (see **Part Five: Historical background**).

FARCICAL COMEDY

The arrival in rapid succession, firstly of Hermia and Lysander, then of Robin, and lastly of Helena and Demetrius, takes us away from the world of enchantment into the world of farce: **comedy** based on such dramatic features as improbable situations, mistaken identities, sexual infidelities and excruciating coincidences. We are amused by Robin's misinterpretation of Hermia and Lysander's sleeping arrangements: he thinks the distance between them indicates Lysander's negative attitude towards her, but we have seen a few moments earlier that it reflects Hermia's care to preserve her virginity until she is legally married.

MOUNTING CONFUSION

The greatest source of comedy in the scene is Lysander's instant transformation from Hermia's lover to Helena's, a transformation which none of the characters, least of all Lysander himself, understands. His claim that it is due to the power of 'reason' (lines 121–2) is hilariously wide of the mark. The joke is capped by Helena's mistaken belief that he is mocking her, which has the **paradoxical** result that the more passionately he tells her that he loves her, the more disgusted with him she becomes. As well as entertaining us in its own right, this situation foreshadows what is likely to occur when Titania awakens, and keeps us looking ahead to that moment. In the event, Shakespeare waits until well into Act III Scene 1, when Titania is finally being pushed out of our thoughts by later developments, before he suddenly brings her back on to the stage, so taking us by surprise.

STUDY FOCUS: THE NATURE OF LOVE (A02)

Lysander claims that love is under the control of intelligence and logic. 'The will of man is by his reason swayed,' he tells Helena, 'And reason says you are the worthier maid' (lines 121–2). This neat **couplet** is clearly inadequate to describe the messy reality of love, which owes more to instinct and emotion than to reason. In the play this irrationality is **symbolised** by the magic juice. When Lysander assures Hermia of his lifelong loyalty (line 69), it is likely that the audience will have guessed what is about to happen and be ready to enjoy the dramatic irony when he abruptly rejects Hermia and switches his allegiance to Helena.

By a further irony, Helena is unable to believe that he loves her. Demetrius's repeated rejections have convinced her that she is unattractive. The more Lysander praises Helena with the language of courtly love, the more she thinks he is insulting her. The more love he expresses, the less loved she feels. Shakespeare amuses us by pushing the irrational behaviour of lovers to an extreme, but abruptly changes the tone when Hermia wakes and finds she has lost Lysander. Hermia's awakening from her nightmare offers a sudden moment of fear, which gives dramatic contrast to the comedy we have witnessed and reminds us that for the participants this is by no means an amusing situation, but one of great anxiety which could lead to highly unpleasant consequences. Her quick exclamations and questions show her loneliness and fear, a reminder that love can make us vulnerable and that for the person concerned it is not at all comical.

REVISION FOCUS: TASK 1 (A02)

How far do you agree with the statements below?

● It is only the presence of the fairies that makes the four lovers' quarrels entertaining.
● The most important source of comedy in the play is dramatic irony.

Try writing opening paragraphs for essays based on these discussion points. Set out your arguments clearly.

GLOSSARY

4	**reremice**	bats
13	**Philomel**	the nightingale
36	**ounce**	lynx
37	**Pard**	leopard
94	**fond**	foolish
110	**Transparent**	bright, pure, without deceit
138	**gentleness**	gentlemanly behaviour

GRADE BOOSTER (A02)

Sound and rhythm are an important part of poetry and you should try to refer to them when you quote. Here the regular, **end-stopped** lines of the lovers' speech make their ideas sound trite, while the short, rhyming lines of the fairies are well suited to magic spells. In contrast, the sudden pauses in Hermia's final speech show her uncertainty and her surges of emotion, suddenly bringing strong human feeling into the play.

EXTENDED COMMENTARY

ACT II SCENE 2 LINES 94–162

In this section of the play we are shown how love may bring misery. Demetrius cannot accept rejection by Hermia; Helena cannot accept rejection by Demetrius. Oberon's well-meaning attempt to help backfires when his assistant Robin misapplies the magic juice to the eyes of Lysander instead of Demetrius, breaking up the previously happy relationship of Hermia and Lysander, and leaving Hermia abandoned by Lysander and Lysander rejected by Helena. The situation would be painful if the lovers' heated and complicated behaviour wasn't so laughable.

We have previously witnessed Helena's degrading pursuit of Demetrius through the wood. She implores him:

> Use me but as your spaniel: spurn me, strike me,
> Neglect me, lose me; only give me leave,
> Unworthy as I am, to follow you. (II.1.205–7)

This is an outrageous reversal of gender roles. Helena's desperate seizure of the initiative is therefore comically unladylike, and this is re-established at the beginning of the present extract, where her being 'out of breath' (II.2.94) suggests that she enters literally chasing Demetrius across the stage.

Since Helena and Demetrius last appeared, Oberon has put the magic juice on the eyes of Titania, and Robin has put it on the eyes of Lysander, mistaking him for Demetrius. Lysander and Hermia continue to sleep on the stage, unseen by Helena, as she abandons her pursuit of Demetrius and stops to reflect. The audience are aware that the two sleepers are nearby and that Lysander is primed to fall in love with the next creature he sees, so we can easily form a hypothesis about what is likely to happen next, and can enjoy the wait to see if we are right. This interest in the larger situation tends to undermine the sadness of Helena's speech, which is also undercut by its neat rhyming **couplets**, its equally neat **antitheses** ('The more my prayer, the lesser is my grace', line 95) and its occasional exaggerations ('I am as ugly as a bear', line 100). All these devices distance us from Helena's emotions and ensure that we look upon her as a comic figure, rather than a badly treated young woman.

Helena's discovery of the sleeping Lysander produces a series of explicit questions ('But who is here? Lysander on the ground? / Dead – or asleep?', lines 106–7) which seem almost to be shared with the audience, as a character might speak in a modern Christmas pantomime. The lines are not far removed from Thisbe's crude declamation later in the play, 'Asleep, my love? / What, dead, my dove?' (V.1.306–7), and the effect, again, is to distance us from Helena's feelings so that we can enjoy what will happen next. What happens, inevitably, is that when she urges, 'Lysander, if you live, good sir, awake!' (line 108) he starts up and declares his love for her with the words, 'And run through fire I will for thy sweet sake' (line 109), his first line rhyming with her previous one to form a decisively comical reply.

Lysander's instant conversion from Hermia's admirer to Helena's is all that we had hoped, or feared. It is pursued regardless of Helena's disconcerted reactions, and rationalised by arguments ('reason says you are the worthier maid', line 122) that are clearly bogus. In trying to account for his changed feelings, Lysander is merely deceiving himself. Because we have all rationalised away the real motives of our behaviour at one time or another, we appreciate the **satire**. However, the main source of humour lies in seeing both characters caught up in a situation beyond their control. Lysander's change of heart is the more entertaining because he has so often professed his love for Hermia. Similarly, Helena has just been lamenting that she is too ugly to be loved when Lysander declares his passion for her. The two are now at total cross-purposes with their earlier statements as well as with each other.

As Helena gradually realises what Lysander means, she becomes more and more angry, interpreting his protestations of love as mockery. Instead of being grateful for his attentions, she scolds him fiercely, repeating her words to emphasise her fury and calling him 'young man' (line 131) to show her disdain, before stalking off stage with all the dignity that, in her anger and self-pity, she can muster. Lysander pauses a moment to address the sleeping Hermia, so that we can see how hostile to her he has become, before going off in futile pursuit of Helena.

There is a strong change of tone when Hermia awakens. The much more varied rhythm of her speech makes it sound like authentic feeling, in contrast to the neatly **end-stopped couplets** of the previous two speakers. The way she repeats Lysander's name shows her reaching out for companionship and protection in the darkness of the wood.

The serpent of her dream is a powerful **symbol** of danger, not only crystallising the vulnerability to wild animals which Hermia feels when she finds herself alone in the wood, but recalling the serpent in Genesis who tempted Eve to betray Adam. The serpent is a symbol of malice throughout the play. The fairies begin the lullaby for their queen by warning off 'spotted snakes with double tongue' (II.2.9) and in his epilogue Robin implores the audience not to respond to the play with 'the serpent's tongue' (V.1.411).

GRADE BOOSTER A02

Shakespeare often uses patterns of **imagery** which recur throughout a play, as the snake image does here. Look out for these series of images and try to comment on their cumulative effect and their relevance to the themes of the story.

The short questions and exclamations which make up most of the second half of Hermia's speech are uttered as she rises and fearfully explores the stage. While we may be confident that everything will come right at the end of the play, her exit still leaves us in considerable suspense. What will she find? Will Helena still be rejecting Lysander? Will Lysander and Demetrius have come to blows? Shakespeare does not answer any of these questions immediately, but leaves them at the backs of our minds, instead taking us to another part of the wood where the craftsmen are just beginning their rehearsals.

ACT III SCENE 1

SUMMARY

- The craftsmen arrive in the wood to discuss and rehearse their play.
- Their performance is disrupted by the mischievous puck Robin, who uses magic to give Bottom the head of an ass.
- After the others have fled in terror, Titania awakens and, under the spell of the magic juice, falls in love with the transformed Bottom.

CONTEXT **A04**

Titania's four attendants are named after natural medicines. Cobwebs were used to staunch blood. Mustardseed was used in a poultice to relieve stiff muscles. The pea plant supplied oil to ease the pain of lost love. Boiled moths were an ingredient of various plasters and potions.

ANALYSIS

PROBLEMS IN REHEARSAL

The craftsmen's assumption that their main problem in putting on a play is that it will be too lifelike is a ridiculous misconception. Bottom, for example, thinks the ladies in the audience will be frightened by the violence; Snout has similar worries about the presence of a lion. Their literal-minded solution (to explain that they are only actors) enhances the joke, and unobtrusively contrasts with Shakespeare's own theatrical skill. In particular, their idea of creating a moonlit scene by bringing on an actor to personify Moonshine stands in direct opposition to the subtle use of language by which Shakespeare creates a moonlight atmosphere throughout *A Midsummer Night's Dream*.

Robin's intervention in the rehearsal guarantees us further fun, and his reference to 'the cradle of the Fairy Queen' (line 61) causes us to remember that Titania is concealed nearby and wonder whether she will be drawn into the events.

STUDY FOCUS: THE CHARACTER OF NICK BOTTOM

The disruption of the rehearsal is a great opportunity for comic action. It also raises Bottom in our estimation. If Bottom's lack of alarm and his playful banter with the fairies reminds us how thick-skinned he is, it equally shows us that he has the knack of accepting whatever happens to him and making the most of it. His observation to Titania that 'reason and love keep little company together nowadays' (lines 120–1) is considerably more perceptive than the self-deceiving speeches we have recently heard from Lysander. It seems that Bottom has not yet realised he has acquired the head of an ass, however, as his use of the words 'ass' and 'ass head' (lines 99 and 97) are amusing precisely because they are unintentionally appropriate. The exact point at which he does realise what has happened is a matter for judgement and has been placed in performance and critical commentary anywhere between this scene and his awakening in Act IV Scene 1.

GLOSSARY

2	**Pat**	right on time
79	**Ninnys'**	fool's
98	**translated**	transformed
109	**cuckoo**	because a cuckoo lays its eggs in other birds' nests, a 'cuckold' was a term used for a husband whose wife had a sexual relationship with another man. Someone who feared he might be a cuckold would naturally find the cuckoo's song a displeasing sound
122	**gleek upon occasion**	make a satirical joke when the opportunity arises
177	**enforcèd**	the meaning is ambiguous. It is usually interpreted as violated or raped, but could actually have the opposite sense of compelled or unwanted

KEY QUOTATIONS: ACT III SCENE 1 A01

Key quotation 1:

Quince explains, 'Pyramus and Thisbe meet by moonlight' (lines 37–8).

Possible interpretations:

- The craftsmen need to find a way of creating an effect of moonlight in their play, which they struggle to achieve.
- Their effort contrasts with Oberon's opening line, 'Ill met by moonlight, proud Titania!' (II.1.60), where Shakespeare is able to achieve the effect they seek simply by his bold, creative use of language.

Key quotation 2:

Bottom complains of his colleagues' panic, 'This is to make an ass of me' (line 99).

Possible interpretations:

- He believes wrongly that they are pretending to be scared in order to make him look like a fool.
- Since the puck has given him the head of an ass, his words are unintentionally appropriate.

Other useful quotations:

Bottom on his own wisdom: 'I can gleek upon occasion' (line 122).

Titania on Bottom: 'Thou art as wise as thou art beautiful' (line 123).

Titania abducts Bottom: 'Thou shalt remain here, whether thou wilt or no' (line 127).

CONTEXT A04

We do not know the design of Bottom's ass head in Shakespeare's original production. The head must look comical and show the transformation clearly, yet still keep the actor's facial expressions visible. This has proved a challenge. The nineteenth century actor Samuel Phelps solved the problem with an ass head of his own, which he took to an 1867 production and wore in preference to the unsatisfactory new one he was offered.

EXTENDED COMMENTARY

ACT III SCENE 1 LINES 1–55

After the quarrels of the fairies and the lovers, the confusion in the woods is increased by the arrival of a third group, the craftsmen. We have previously seen them planning a play for the wedding celebration (Act I Scene 2). Now they meet in the wood to begin their rehearsal, but it soon becomes clear that there are technical problems to be resolved before it can take place. The audience know, though the craftsmen do not, that the wood also holds the fairies and the lovers, and are therefore not altogether surprised when the puck enters shortly after Bottom's last speech and decides to enliven the proceedings. (In the First Folio, he is indicated as entering twice, the first time at line 41, when Bottom is shouting 'Find out moonshine!' It may be that in productions of Shakespeare's time he did come in and haunt the men invisibly, before coming forward to speak to the audience at line 60.)

Bottom's opening question, 'Are we all met?' (line 1) suggests he may be the last to arrive; otherwise he would know who was there. It is typical of the ebullience for which he is known as 'Bully Bottom' (line 7) that he at once takes the initiative, but he is careful to work through the chairmanship of Peter Quince, who seems to be the originator of the project and has the more methodical, detailed approach to it. It is Quince, for example, who chooses the location for their rehearsal. The place is 'marvellous convenient' (line 2) because the features are exactly what he says they are. The 'green plot' (line 3) is an ideal stage because it is the stage of the theatre, while the 'hawthorn brake' is the actual dressing room area.

Just as Bottom held up the proceedings in Act I Scene 2, so he now prevents the rehearsal beginning by objecting that the drawing of a sword on stage will frighten the women in the audience. It has been suggested that this fear reflects violent unrest among workers during the 1590s, which would have made the upper classes especially sensitive to a working man drawing a sword in their presence, but there is no evidence in the play that anyone finds this particular set of workers alarming. Rather the opposite. The craftsmen are looked down upon and laughed at by aristocrats and fairies alike.

The craftsmen's fear that the nobles will mistake Bottom and Snug for a valiant hero and a wild lion is funny precisely because they place such great faith in their own acting abilities and so little importance on the willing participation of the audience in the illusion. Plainly anyone who goes to the theatre knows that what they are about to witness is art, not 'life'. It is true that they might at times become so caught up in what they see that their emotional reactions become similar to those of everyday reality, but it requires considerable dramatic experience to bring this about – considerably more than Quince and company possess. The craftsmen's naïveté is so great, however, that Starveling even suggests leaving out the death of Pyramus altogether.

Bottom's constructive solution to the problem is to equip the play with an introduction or prologue which will reassure the audience that their **tragedy** is only an imitation of life. He is so enthusiastic that he wants the speech written in 'eight and eight' (line 20),

---

CONTEXT A04

Food shortages caused considerable unrest during the 1590s. In 1595, a weaver who called for the death of the queen was locked up as mad, but rescued by other workers, who then stole food and began a riot. Later in the year martial law was declared and six workmen were hanged.

CONTEXT A04

Snout's question, 'Will the ladies not be afeard of the lion?' (line 21) may recall a real event. In 1594, when Prince Henry was baptised at the Scottish court, a plan to bring in a chariot drawn by a lion was abandoned because the animal might frighten those at the front and have been spooked by the flaming torches that lit the room.

not a mere 'eight and six' (line 19), not realising that the figures only represent the number of syllables per line. Naturally, Bottom assumes that he will play the part of the prologue, so that his suggestion has the secondary benefit of giving him another role in the play. In the event, although Quince agrees to the suggestion, he manages to reallocate the part to himself before the performance.

A second objection comes from Snout, that the presence of a lion on stage may cause the female members of the audience just as much alarm as a sword. Bottom is quick to take up the point and elaborate it, showing again that he is the most confident speaker among the craftsmen. As usual, much of the humour in this scene comes from pretentious misuse of language. The lion is a fierce wild beast, not a 'fearful … wildfowl' (line 25), and Snug should be speaking to the same effect, not 'the same defect' (line 30), although this phrase may be an accurate description of his timid delivery.

Having accepted this second revision of the script, Quince himself raises problems. The first is to 'bring the moonlight into a chamber' (line 37). His fellow craftsmen suggest opening the window so the moonlight can shine in, provided the moon shines on the wedding night. They speak of looking up the date in an almanac – a book of dates, listing significant occasions such as anniversaries and astronomical events – but Quince's confident announcement that 'it doth shine that night' (line 42) need not involve him consulting a book. He may well have looked up the date earlier. In any case, he has a more dramatically satisfying solution ready than the simple opening of a window. One of the actors can act the part of Moonshine. His choice of the word 'disfigure' (line 47) here is again comically appropriate, as Starveling, equipped with the traditional props of a lantern, a thorn bush and a dog, gives a very poor impression of magical, transforming light. In contrast, Shakespeare's many references to the moon and moonlight subtly create a night-time world where anything may prove possible.

Quince's second problem, how to bring a wall on stage, is dealt with in the same manner. An actor will play the wall. This time Bottom is first to propose the solution (though we may suspect that he snatches the words from Quince's mouth) and, with his love of theatrical detail, he rejoices in envisaging the appropriate costume. Again, we may note how, in comparison, Shakespeare can create a palace and a wood on stage simply by the suggestive power of his language, and can create patterns of opposition and marrying together throughout the play without the need of physical walls to make the point clear.

CONTEXT **A04**

If the puck does enter invisibly at line 41, as the First Folio indicates, what does he do on stage? Directors have given him a range of comic business, including tickling the craftsmen, annoying them with a sneezing spell and borrowing Quince's script to find out about their play.

REVISION FOCUS: TASK 2 A03

How far do you agree with the statements below?

- Robin Goodfellow's pranks are more cruel than amusing.
- The craftsmen are mere stereotypes whom we are expected to look down upon.

Try writing opening paragraphs for essays based on these discussion points. Set out your arguments clearly.

ACT III SCENE 2

SUMMARY

- Robin tells Oberon about the trick he has played on the craftsmen and assures him that he has also solved the problem of the lovers.
- Oberon soon sees that Robin's intervention has misfired. In a second attempt to help, he sends Robin to fetch Helena while he himself puts the magic juice on Demetrius's eyes.
- Demetrius and Lysander now become rivals for Helena's love, while she believes that both of them are tormenting her, probably with the connivance of Hermia, who joins them during the quarrel.
- To prevent violence, Oberon orders Robin to intervene again, drawing the lovers apart. Once they have grown weary and fallen asleep, Robin puts an antidote juice on Lysander's eyes to take away his love for Helena.

CHECK THE FILM **A03**

The lovers' confrontations are commonly enhanced by physical comedy. In both the 1981 BBC production and the 1999 film version, the descent of Hermia and Helena from civilised women to brawlers ends with one or both toppling into a large pool of mud, giving added force to Helena's anguished cry, 'O excellent!' (line 247).

ANALYSIS

CONFUSION ALL ROUND

Throughout this scene the audience derive a great amount of enjoyment from knowing more than the characters. Not one of the lovers fully understands what is going on and we are entertained by their astonishment when they suddenly learn that all is not as they had thought. When Robin enters, we share his jollity as he summarises for Oberon the results of his pranks, incidentally allowing Shakespeare to recreate Robin's disruption of the rehearsal in such a way as to draw the best possible picture of it for the audience, but we know that Robin's confidence that he has solved the problem of the young Athenians will soon prove to be misplaced. Even as he is speaking, Hermia and Demetrius are coming on stage and Robin turns from being the instigator of misunderstanding to yet another victim of it, as the object of Oberon's anger.

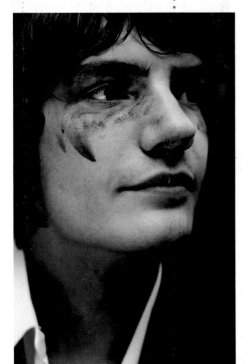

The confrontation between Hermia and Demetrius, which out of its context might seem painful and ominous, becomes amusing for us because we know that the whole dispute is misconceived and temporary, a point reinforced by the presence of Oberon and Robin whom we can count upon to put it right. Oberon's subsequent anger and Robin's rather anxious compliance with his orders ('I go, I go – look how I go –', line 100) constitute a second comic double-act, which gives us a respite from the lovers' confusion. However, the arrival of Helena and Lysander, followed by the return of Hermia, escalates the degree of misunderstandings between the four lovers to a comic crescendo, which achieves the maximum amount of confusion between them.

WHO LOVES WHOM?

Not observing his rival asleep nearby, Lysander reminds Helena that Demetrius loves Hermia. At this very moment Demetrius starts up and extravagantly declares his love for Helena instead. The more Lysander and Demetrius insist upon their love for Helena, the more rejected by them she feels and the more angry and contemptuous she becomes. The more Hermia is insulted by Lysander and Demetrius, the more Helena believes her to be in league with them. Hermia, meanwhile, is soon convinced of the opposite, that the others are in league against her, and a total breakdown of relationships is reached.

STUDY FOCUS: LIGHT AND DARK ⒶO2

The subject matter of comedy is often distressing. If we were to look at the story through the eyes of the jealous and frustrated lovers lost in the wood, the terrified craftsmen running back to Athens pursued by supernatural apparitions, or even the bickering fairy king and queen, we might think there was little to laugh about. We are able to experience their distress as funny because we see them from the outside, do not empathise too closely with them and are confident that everything will turn out for the best in the end.

In the case of the four lovers in particular, comedy is preserved by the benevolent presence of Oberon, who explains to Robin how things may be put right with such confidence that we have no fear of a **tragic** ending. Robin speaks with sinister **imagery**: 'dragons … ghosts … wormy beds … black-browed night' (lines 379–87), which probably echoes what the original audience would have associated with fairies, but Oberon responds by characterising himself and the other good spirits with contrastingly healthy country **imagery**. This adds to the sense that we are moving towards a positive conclusion. We are both relieved and entertained as we see Robin tricking the four into behaving as he wishes before commenting on the happy outcome in rustic terms ('The man shall have his mare again', line 463) that follow on from the natural **images** used by Oberon.

CHECK THE BOOK ⒶO3

Shakespeare's comedy *The Merry Wives of Windsor*, which is thought to have been written a few years after *A Midsummer Night's Dream*, includes a scene where several characters carry out a revenge attack disguised as fairies. The pinching, burning and supernatural threats which they employ suggest that Robin's sinister description of fairies was a common view.

GLOSSARY

17	**nole**	head
28	**senseless**	inanimate
30	**From yielders all things catch**	everything is torn from those who have lost control
188	**oes and eyes**	stars
203	**artificial**	skilful
213	**like coats in heraldry**	the two girls were united as the coats of arms of a man and a woman were combined under one crest when they married
220/344	**amazed**	confused, as though lost in a maze
317	**simple and … fond**	foolish
355	**Hie**	go
356	**welkin**	sky
357	**Acheron**	a river in Hades (Hell)
380	**Aurora's harbinger**	the dawn's herald, the morning star

EXTENDED COMMENTARY

ACT III SCENE 2 LINES 345–412

The four lovers have reached the point of greatest confusion. Both Lysander and Demetrius have had the magic juice put on their eyes and, as a result, have fallen for Helena and rejected Hermia. They regard this as entirely natural behaviour, but the two women are baffled. Helena assumes that the men are making fun of her, concluding that this must be because Hermia has told them to do so. Hermia meanwhile, after her initial disbelief at Lysander's alteration, has become convinced that Helena must have seduced him away from her and in reaction she tries to physically assault her rival. Violence also springs up between the men. Intending to fight over who shall have Helena, Lysander and Demetrius stride off to find a suitable place to hold a duel. Helena then runs fearfully from Hermia, who pursues her, though by this time more in bafflement than in anger.

After the rhyming **couplets** of Helena and Hermia, Oberon's first two unrhyming lines create a minor irregularity in the sound of the **verse** which signals the return to dramatic prominence of himself and the puck. They may have been off-stage during the argument between the lovers, but more likely have been positioned to one side. Just as we have been entertained by the chaotic relationships of the lovers, so we are entertained by the confusion of the fairy king, whose efforts to help the humans have only made the situation worse.

In the present scene Oberon and Robin become a double act, with Oberon taking the part of the 'straight man', scolding the puck for his bungled mission. In some productions Oberon takes hold of the puck or pushes him round the stage. The

incorrigible Robin, though defensive at first, rapidly shifts the blame back on to Oberon (whose orders he has, after all, followed to the letter) and is unrepentant about enjoying the outcome of his error as much as we in the audience have done. He addresses Oberon as 'King of shadows' (line 347) because the fairies are mysterious creatures, active in the night. However, the phrase also anticipates Theseus's description of actors as shadows (V.1.205), and eventually Robin will bring the two meanings together in his epilogue with the phrase 'we shadows' (see the section on **Theatre** in **Part Three: Themes**).

Oberon's long speech beginning, 'Thou seest these lovers' (line 354), is a highly reassuring one, which takes much of the suspense out of the story. It is unusual to be told so far from the conclusion that characters will live happily ever after. Oberon even seems sure that Titania will let him have the little boy who was the object of their quarrel, and in forecasting that for the lovers 'all this derision / Shall seem a dream' (lines 370–1) he predicts the epilogue, where Robin says much the same about the whole play. Clearly Shakespeare no longer wishes us to be in suspense about the outcome of the lovers' conflicts. Having been brought to the point of maximum tension, these will be resolved and new sources of dramatic interest be brought in to replace them.

The decisiveness and confidence with which Oberon speaks is typical of his supernatural authority. The comparatively heavy **end-stopping** of these lines gives them the chanted rhythm of a spell. Some of the **imagery** has a sinister quality which adds to the seriousness of tone: 'black as Acheron … death-counterfeiting sleep / With leaden legs and batty wings' (lines 357–65). This tone is picked up and amplified in the puck's reply with its gruesome references to 'ghosts' (line 381) and their 'wormy beds' (line 384). However, this proves to be an opportunity for Oberon to emphasise that the fairies are 'spirits of another sort' (line 388). If they are not at home in the full glare of daylight, they are at least able to continue their activities for the duration of dawn, unlike evil spirits who cannot bear any sunlight. A Protestant who believed in the existence of fairies would be hard pressed to account for their origin without explaining them as disguised demons. Where could they come from but Hell? Shakespeare is anxious that we see the fairies positively, as **personifications** of the forces of nature, and appropriately Oberon himself now employs personification. Robin has already spoken of the dawn as the goddess Aurora. Oberon goes on to claim that he has exercised his masculine charms on her, and speaks of the sea in the form of the sea god Neptune.

Does the puck sing or speak the next lines: 'Up and down, up and down,/ I will lead them up and down' (lines 396–7)? As on several other occasions when Robin or the fairies shift their speech into short rhyming lines, it would be possible to sing them, either with or without musical accompaniment. They certainly mark a transition from conversation to enchantment, and we can now sit back and enjoy the trickery through which Robin draws the two young men apart.

The type of stage on which actors performed in the Elizabethan era made little use of scenery (see **Part Five: Historical background**). It was possible, therefore, to change locations, or split the stage between several locations, by the use of language alone. When Lysander enters, we do not have to assume that he is wandering back into the place he had left earlier. Robin can move towards him, indicating that he is moving to a different part of the wood to find him. Similarly, when Lysander leaves and Demetrius appears, Robin can race over to him. As the puck dances around the two men, calling out to each in turn, their acting and the imagination of the audience furnish the bare stage with the bushes of which they speak. In our mind's eye we see Robin hiding behind branches and the two rivals clambering through an intricate forest. In film and television productions, the puck is able to imitate perfectly the voices of his two victims by lip-synching to tapes of them. On stage it is easy enough for him to approximate

their voices and the other two actors to respond accordingly. Whatever our reservations about the tricks Robin plays on Titania and Bottom, we enjoy seeing the two young men who have rejected Hermia (and, in the case of Demetrius, Helena) tormented and misled.

CHECK THE BOOK **A03**

In Shakespeare's tragedy *Hamlet*, the ghost of Hamlet's father appears at night and demands that his son revenges his murder. As soon as the dawn comes, the ghost flees to the tomb. Clearly Shakespeare intended the fairies of *A Midsummer Night's Dream*, who can tolerate at least some daylight, to be much less sinister.

ACT IV SCENE 1

SUMMARY

- Oberon and Robin remove the magic spells from Titania and Bottom. Oberon and Titania are reunited.
- Theseus and his companions, out early in the morning, discover the four sleeping lovers, who explain their changed feelings.
- Theseus overrules the objections of Egeus and declares that the two young couples shall be married alongside him and Hippolyta.
- When everyone else has left, Bottom awakens and reflects on his strange 'dream'.

ANALYSIS

LOVED BY A QUEEN

The dalliance of Titania and Bottom **parodies** what must have been every Elizabethan man's daydream, to be loved by a queen and waited upon by her servants. Bottom adopts the courtly French term 'Monsieur' (line 7), but cannot conceal his hairy face, big ears and primitive taste in music ('the tongs and the bones', lines 26–7). Even as we are amused, we are nonetheless likely to be moved by Titania's adoration of him and to be reminded yet again that love is in the eye of the beholder.

BACK TO NORMAL

When Oberon and Robin enter and restore the normal order of things, we are pleased to see the king and queen of the fairies reunited, especially since we know that their relationship is **symbolic** of harmony in nature, yet it is difficult not to resent Oberon's treatment of Titania. Throughout the play he seems confident of his right to interfere in the lives of others. Here he tricks and humiliates his wife when she will not give him what he wants, then casually orders her to be silent ('Silence awhile!', line 79). This is an extreme image of masculine control. In keeping with the play's fondness for pairings, however, the presence of the dominating spirit Oberon is balanced by that of the grotesque Bottom, a man who has achieved happiness and respect only because a woman's love has lifted him above himself. Oberon is the more impressive figure, but he is not after all a human being as Bottom is.

The king and queen of the fairies dance in celebration of their reunion, Oberon promising that they will dance again tomorrow, blessing Theseus's house after his marriage. The dance of Oberon and Titania symbolises the restoration of the order of nature, pictured for centuries as a cosmic dance of the elements.

NEXT MORNING

After this musical interlude, Robin and Theseus use the **imagery** of morning and daylight to lead us back into the normal world where the court party finds the four young lovers sleeping. The baying of the dogs, each noisy, but together forming a harmony ('so musical a discord, such sweet thunder', line 115), seems to parallel the way that **comedy** takes disturbing, disruptive events and resolves them into a pleasing unity, and so signals to the audience that we are moving towards the conclusion of the play. Certainly the ranting of Egeus, reluctantly respected by Theseus in Act I Scene 1, is dismissed out of hand here. Theseus reverses his earlier decision and permits a happy ending. Characteristically, Shakespeare is unconcerned with probability or realism at this turning point of the story.

STUDY FOCUS: BOTTOM'S DREAM SPEECH A03

It is left to Bottom to comment on what has taken place during the night. He comes up with a garbled variation on a passage from the Bible, another example of how the play brings together opposites, in this case the solemn words of scripture, scrambled and applied to the experiences of a comical character. In the Bishops' Bible, the translation known to Shakespeare, the relevant words are, 'The eye hath not seen, and the ear hath not heard, neither have entered into the heart of man, the things which God hath prepared for them that love him' (1 Corinthians 2:9). Although we are not expected to take the antics of the fairies too seriously, they are one way of conceiving the cosmic forces which drive existence and empower love, and in his way Bottom has glimpsed something of this. Unfortunately, his ability to express it is limited to an ill-conceived '**ballad**', which he proposes to insert into 'Pyramus and Thisbe' in the place where it will do the most damage to the drama.

GLOSSARY

19	**neaf** fist
29	**peck** a measure equivalent to two gallons
137	**Saint Valentine** birds were supposed to choose their mates on St Valentine's Day, 14 February
186	**parted** out of focus with each other

KEY QUOTATIONS: ACT IV SCENE 1 A01

Key quotation 1:

Demetrius: 'It seems to me / That yet we sleep, we dream.' (lines 190–1).

Possible interpretations:

- The lovers have been left in a daze by their experiences.
- The events in the wood have had a permanent influence on their minds.
- In the case of the one who is speaking, Demetrius, Oberon has left the magic juice on his eyes to ensure that he remains in love with Helena.

Key quotation 2:

Bottom: 'it shall be called 'Bottom's Dream', because it hath no bottom' (lines 208–9).

Possible interpretations:

- The song will describe experiences which are so deep that they cannot be explained.
- The song will describe events which are only from a dream, so they have no foundation in reality.
- In order to avoid embarrassment, Bottom will not mention that the ass was actually him – his account will have no bottom in it.

Other useful quotations:

Harmony from conflict: 'So musical a discord, such sweet thunder' (line 115).

Theseus backs true love: 'Egeus, I will overbear your will' (line 17).

CONTEXT A04

The Bishops' Bible was a version of the Bible first published in 1568 and revised in 1572, edited by Archbishop Matthew Parker and other clerics. Because of inconsistencies and inaccuracies in the translation, it was replaced in 1611 by the King James Bible, often called the Authorised Version.

CRITICAL VIEWPOINT A03

How we evaluate Bottom is crucial to our overall view of the play. Is he simply a likeable idiot or does he have qualities which somehow make him more admirable than many of the other characters? His mangled quotation comes from St Paul's comments on the impossibility of understanding God through human reason. Some critics think this indicates that Bottom's positive spirit is a more valuable quality than mere cleverness.

ACT IV SCENE 2

SUMMARY

- The craftsmen are upset about losing Bottom in the haunted wood.
- He suddenly arrives to announce that all is well and their play can be staged after all.

ANALYSIS

BOTTOM'S RETURN

We are able to enjoy the disappointment of the craftsmen because, once again knowing more than they do, we confidently expect Bottom to appear suddenly and change the atmosphere. We are not disappointed.

Bottom is characteristically torn between boasting of his adventures and keeping them a tantalising mystery which will hold the others' attention upon him – or is it perhaps that he wants to tell them his experiences, but does not know how to put them into words? In any case, he has more urgent news, that 'Pyramus and Thisbe' is 'preferred' (line 29). This seems to mean only that the play has been accepted by Philostrate, the Master of the Revels, as a possible entertainment, since Theseus does not finally decide upon it until the next scene. Bottom, however, is full of confidence and the audience can have little doubt that the play will now be staged.

STUDY FOCUS: VERSE AND PROSE   A02

The upper class characters speak mostly in **verse**. The underlying rhythm of the **iambic pentameter** makes their speech sound superior, a style of language that is measured, thoughtful and eloquent. The craftsmen, in contrast, speak in **prose**, which sounds much less distinguished. They not only make greater use of everyday expressions but frequently get their choice of words wrong.

The language of the play reflects the class divisions of the time, but it would be wrong to assume that it consistently supports them. Sometimes the upper class characters say foolish things, while Bottom can be shrewd in his comments as well as positive in his feelings. Look out for moments when language subverts class stereotypes. In Act V, in particular, we will see the craftsmen attempt their own play in verse, while the upper-class characters are reduced to onlookers making mean-spirited comments in prose.

REVISION FOCUS: TASK 3   A03

How far do you agree with the statements below?

- The story finishes with Act IV and logically the play should end there too.
- The problems with which the play begins vanish without any satisfactory explanation in Act IV.

Try writing opening paragraphs for essays based on these discussion points. Set out your arguments clearly.

GLOSSARY

2	**transported**	abducted by supernatural forces
28	**pumps**	light, low-soled shoes

CONTEXT   A04

Flute thinks Bottom might be given a pension of sixpence per day if the play is a success. (There is no doubt about it in the 1999 film version, as the prize is announced on a poster.) That sum would have roughly doubled Bottom's income, so would have made it worth his while to act his heart out.

CONTEXT   A04

The Master of the Revels was a court official who was in charge of organising and supervising royal festivities.

GRADE BOOSTER   A02

The drama starts with the question of who will marry whom, so it would be logical if it ended when this issue has been resolved. Instead, there is a whole fifth act, devoted to the craftsmen's play and the fairies' blessing. Baffled by this, some early productions simply left out Act V or placed 'Pyramus and Thisbe' earlier in the play. Why do you think Shakespeare chose to end the play in the way he did?

ACT V SCENE 1

SUMMARY

- Theseus believes the lovers' adventures happened only in their imaginations.
- He agrees to the staging of 'Pyramus and Thisbe' to celebrate the three weddings. The play is badly written and acted, but these defects only add to its entertainment value.
- When all the humans have gone to bed, the fairies enter the house and bless those who reside there and their children to come. Robin remains behind to deliver an epilogue.

ANALYSIS

IMAGINATION

Theseus's description of lovers, poets and madmen as similarly deluded is amusing but unfair, since creative writers are able to distinguish between their own imaginings and the external world, and most lovers are 'frantic' (line 10) only in valuing the person they love more highly than others do, not in experiencing hallucinations about them. Since Theseus himself is a lover, his remarks to Hippolyta seem somewhat tactless. His remarks about poetry are unlikely to impress an audience who have enjoyed and appreciated the fairy world created by Shakespeare. The fairies are not the products of a defective brain, but skilful art. Neither their author nor the audience believe them to be literally real, but they may believe them to have a 'strange and admirable' significance (line 27) within the context of the play. Hippolyta is more impressed than Theseus by the lovers' testimony, noting its consistency and conviction.

ENTERTAINMENT

Philostrate offers Theseus four pieces of entertainment. The first three, with their **themes** of violence, poverty and death, are clearly unsuitable for a wedding celebration. The initial offering is perhaps the worst. Not only is it to be presented by the inappropriate figure of a eunuch (a castrated man), but as an educated Elizabethan would probably have known, Theseus himself took part in the gruesome battle with the Centaurs and, in so doing, disrupted a wedding feast. After these ill-judged proposals, the **paradoxical** claims made for 'Pyramus and Thisbe', apparently caused by Quince's

uncertain vocabulary ('*tedious brief ... tragical mirth*', lines 56–7), seem refreshingly intriguing. Hippolyta's concern that the actors may be humiliated shows us her caring nature, and Theseus, too, although his account of how he deals with tongue-tied dignitaries might be considered boastful, is lifted in our estimation by his care for others and his perception that glib speeches and sincerity do not always go together.

CONTEXT A04

It was a common complaint of dramatists in Shakespeare's time that some upper class members of the audience liked to show off by making loudly patronising and offensive comments about the performance that they were watching. Shakespeare's friend and rival playwright Ben Jonson called them 'fastidious impertinents'.

INTERRUPTIONS

After Theseus's thoughtful remarks, it is disconcerting to see that he, Hippolyta, Lysander and Demetrius do in fact make sarcastic comments throughout the performance, many if not all of them audible to the actors. Moonshine, in particular, has his contribution ruined by carping interruptions. (Hippolyta's 'I am aweary of this moon. Would he would change', line 238, oddly echoes Theseus's sentiments in the opening lines of the play, bringing us full circle.) It may be that Elizabethan audiences did commonly behave in this way, and that we should take this example as comparatively restrained. In any case, it gives Bottom the chance to show his mettle. Instead of trying to ignore the comments, he boldly steps out of role and explains to the audience, in as patronising a manner as their own, what it is they are supposed to be appreciating.

FEMALE REACTIONS

Back in role, Bottom throws himself into the part of Pyramus with such enthusiasm that Hippolyta cannot help feeling sorry for the character. Unlike the others, Hermia and Helena do not join in the mockery of the play. Would it be impolite for them as 'mere women' to join in with the men and the duchess, or are they perhaps still subdued by the experiences which they have recently gone through, being rejected and insulted by the men they love?

STUDY FOCUS: PYRAMUS AND THISBE A02

'Pyramus and Thisbe' is a masterpiece of incompetence. Quince delivers the Prologue so badly that he manages to consistently reverse its meaning. After that we encounter mispronunciation ('Ninny's tomb', line 197), padded lines ('At the which let no man wonder', line 133), extravagant repetitions ('die, die, die, die, die', line 290), inept **personifications** ('Thanks, courteous wall', line 175), crude **alliteration** ('Quail, crush, conclude, and quell', line 271), ill-chosen **metaphors** and **similes** ('His eyes were green as leeks', line 317), incongruities of tone ('O dear!', line 265) and garbled references to mythology. The short lines used at the **tragic** climax of the play speed up the rhythm and emphasise the rhymes in a way suitable only for **comedy**. There are numerous splendid opportunities for bad acting which different productions will develop in their own ways. Amidst all the comedy, 'Pyramus and Thisbe' does have an underlying seriousness, however. Its story, paralleling that of Romeo and Juliet, shows how young love which defies parental authority can lead to destruction. Lysander and Demetrius, as they laugh at the play, fail to recall how close they came to killing each other on a similar moonlit night only twenty-four hours before. The play concludes with singing and dancing, which creates a sense of celebration and natural harmony.

BLESSING

Theseus's remark that it is almost 'fairy time' (line 342) is probably his joke at the young lovers' expense. However, no sooner has he left the stage than the fairies do enter, reunited, to bless the three marriages. Robin again introduces dark, ghostly **imagery**, but typically of the play, this is soon set aside in favour of the reassuring, domestic imagery of fireplaces and beds. The four lovers whom Egeus originally marched on to

the stage as children have left the stage as adults and are now themselves about to become parents. Oberon concludes the main part of the play by blessing them and their children to come.

THE FINAL SPEECH

When Oberon has finished, Robin's remarks switch the focus of our attention from the events on stage to the relationship between play and audience, inviting us to decide how we shall come to terms with *A Midsummer Night's Dream* and how we shall assess it. Is our experience of it as idle as a dream or something more serious? Does it deserve hissing ('the serpent's tongue', line 411) or applause ('your hands', line 415)?

GLOSSARY

11	**a brow of Egypt**	the dark-skinned face of a gypsy
32	**masques**	spectacular courtly entertainments featuring drama and dance
48	**Bacchanals**	women of Thrace who followed the cult of Bacchus, the god of wine, and in a drunken ecstasy tore to pieces the poet-musician Orpheus
52	**thrice three Muses**	the nine goddesses of the arts
80	**conned**	learned
90	**take what they mistake**	accept positively, and correct in our minds, what they get wrong
96	**periods**	full stops
161	**sinister**	left
191–4	**Limander … Helen … Shafalus … Procrus**	mistakes for Leander, Hero, Cephalus and Procris
229	**horns on his head**	a 'cuckold,' who was deceived by his wife, was supposed to acquire horns on his head
268	**Furies**	supernatural creatures who pursued the guilty in search of vengeance
269	**Fates**	three goddesses in Greek mythology who in turn spun the thread of life, drew it out and finally cut it
270	**Cut thread and thrum**	cut the weaver's thread and its tufted end, i.e. both the good and the valueless, the whole of his life
318	**sisters three**	the Fates
334	**Bergomask dance**	a country dance
362	**triple Hecate**	the goddess called Diana on Earth was known in the heavens as Luna, Phoebe or Cynthia, and in Hell as Proserpina or Hecate

CONTEXT **A04**

Shakespeare's plays have few stage directions, but a remark in Edward Sharpham's play *The Fleire*, dating from the 1600s, seems to refer to Shakespeare's original production. When Thisbe came to kill herself, she was unable to find Pyramus's sword and was reduced to stabbing herself to death with the scabbard.

KEY QUOTATIONS: ACT V SCENE 1   **A01**

Key quotation 1:

Theseus says of the amateur actors, 'The best in this kind are but shadows' (line 205).

Possible interpretations:

● Even the best actors are only imitators of reality, so what they do should not be taken seriously (this seems to be Theseus's intended meaning).

● Since actors imitate reality, their plays must show us something valid about our lives.

● Like the fairies, who are also called 'shadows' (III.2.347 and V.1.401), the actors can draw us into a mysterious world where our sense of ourselves can be transformed.

Key quotation 2:

Titania says the lovers' story 'grows to something of great constancy' (line 26).

Possible interpretations:

● Their stories are so consistent that there must be some truth to them.

● Their experiences have led them to a love in which they will all be true to one another.

CHARACTERS

THE THREE GROUPS

The characters in *A Midsummer Night's Dream* can be divided into three groups. The first to appear on stage are the Athenian nobles, who soon divide themselves up into the four lovers and the rest of the court. Next, the Athenian craftsmen make an appearance; finally, the fairies. Although there is some interaction between them as the story unfolds, the three groups remain remarkably distinct throughout the play.

HIERARCHY

One major area of difference between the groups lies in their comparative status and power, which is reflected in how much they know about each other. The craftsmen, at the bottom of the hierarchy, have no insight into or power over the higher groups, while the nobles and the fairies can readily watch, comment upon and influence them. Elevated above the nobles by their supernatural powers, the fairies are also able to monitor them and intervene in their affairs, while the nobles in return are barely aware of the fairies' existence. In the position of greatest superiority, Oberon and his assistant Robin are the most powerful members of the fairy group, observing and controlling everyone – including the fairy queen, Titania – and making themselves invisible to all but the theatre audience whenever they wish.

TRANSFORMATIONS

Each of the three groups is made up, for the most part, of characters who are fixed in role. Only Nick Bottom and the puck Robin Goodfellow have a playful desire to experience others' identities which allows them to cross temporarily from their own group to another one. Robin can imitate anything animal, vegetable or human, including the voices of Lysander and Demetrius, while Bottom finds himself drawn into the world of the fairies by Robin's spells where he even usurps Oberon's place as Titania's lover.

Oberon and Robin can let us know that they have become invisible simply by announcing the fact. Since one acting company of the 1590s had an invisibility robe listed among its props, it could also be that Shakespeare's actors made use of a similar item to add visual flair to their vanishing tricks.

CRITICAL VIEWPOINT A03

The four lovers have somewhat limited developments as characters, but this helps to make their changes of allegiance dramatically effective, since there is so little to choose between them. More personality would only have complicated our reactions. Do you agree?

STUDY FOCUS: DOUBLING THE PARTS   A04

On stage it is possible to create more overlap between the groups by following Bottom's wish in Act I Scene 2 and having actors take more than one part. It is impossible to know how such matters would have been dealt with in Shakespeare's original productions, but since the 1960s Theseus and Oberon have often been played by the same actor and Hippolyta and Titania by the same actress. Peter Brooks's 1970 version also cast the same actor as Philostrate and the puck. When such pairings are made, they inevitably affect our interpretation of the play. The doublings cited above, for example, suggest that the fairy world is in some sense a projection of the Athenians' group subconscious, with the fairies as dream-selves of the mortals, manifesting and working out their mixed feelings towards each other in fantasy form through the night.

THESEUS

WHO IS THESEUS?

- The conqueror of the Amazons, who is about to marry their queen, Hippolyta.
- The ruler of Athens, who must decide the fate of Hermia when she refuses to marry her father's choice of husband.

ONCE A HERO

Theseus is a figure from Greek mythology. Before the audience see him on stage they are likely to already know him by reputation as a great hero, famous for such deeds as the slaying of the Minotaur. In defiance of such expectations, his actions within the play are not those of a heroic warrior, but of a respectable, middle-aged gentleman. Despite a number of references to his legendary past, Theseus cuts a distinctly unromantic figure, sober in action, moderate (even complacent) in tone, and positively scornful of lovers' passions and 'antique fables' (V.1.3). He is always well-meaning and sensible, restraining the excesses of Egeus, giving eventual support to the lovers, presiding over the marriage festivities and rewarding the craftsmen for their dramatic efforts. In all this he is far from the ruthless killer and faithless lover of legend.

STILL A HERO?

How far should we allow our knowledge of Theseus outside the play to affect our response to him within it? Oberon's reference to his promiscuous past (II.1.77–80) ensures that we cannot ignore the point. Shakespeare probably intends Theseus's departure from his heroic legend to be an incidental comic feature of the play, but some recent critics have suggested that the duke is a man under whose respectable surface lurk exotic knowledge and passions which have been repressed only temporarily.

CONTEXT A04

The Minotaur was a monster with the head of a bull and the body of a man, which Minos, the King of Crete, kept in a maze-like underground prison, the Labyrinth. The king fed the monster young Athenians until Theseus killed it and escaped with the help of Minos's daughter, Ariadne.

STUDY FOCUS: A MALE TYRANT? A03

Many modern readers see Theseus as a figure of patriarchal authority. He has defeated a nation of female warriors, the Amazons. Their queen, Hippolyta, seems to be marrying him with little enthusiasm, suggesting that theirs may be a political marriage, not a love match. It is true that Theseus is unhappy about Egeus's treatment of his daughter Hermia and is ready to listen to her side of the argument, but he is reluctant to contradict Egeus's authority and when, in the end, he does permit Hermia and Lysander to marry, the decision is an assertion of his will, not a concession that they have any right to choose for themselves. As a stereotypical man of action, Theseus speaks with contempt of the imagination and poetry (V.1.2-17). This feminist reading of Theseus makes sense when we reflect on the text, but is much harder to bring out when the play is acted, due to his polite, gentlemanly manner which makes the audience see him positively.

KEY QUOTATION: THESEUS A01

Theseus tells Hippolyta: 'I wooed thee with my sword, / And won thy love doing thee injuries; / But I will wed thee in another key' (I.1.16–18).

Possible interpretations:

- Theseus defeated Hippolyta in battle, but now he wishes to love and respect her.
- The movement from discord to concord is typical of his attitude and sets the tone of the whole play.
- To feminists, Theseus is a domineering male who thinks he can cover up and legitimise his violence with a show of friendship.

CRITICAL VIEWPOINT A03

For G. Wilson Knight, Theseus has put his youthful adventures behind him and become the 'calmest and wisest' of the characters with 'an exquisite and wide love and deep human knowledge'. More recently, for Shirley Nelson Garner, Theseus remains a 'lover-and-leaver of women' who, having abducted Hippolyta, naturally sympathises with Demetrius's desire to force Hermia into marriage. Which of these views do you think is the more convincing?

HIPPOLYTA

WHO IS HIPPOLYTA?

● Hippolyta is the queen of the Amazons, defeated in battle by Theseus.
● She is now marrying Theseus, but never shows enthusiasm when she speaks to him and may be marrying him as part of a peace treaty.

AMAZON OR OBEDIENT WIFE?

Hippolyta, like Theseus, is a more elusive character than she may at first appear. Her evident concern for Hermia in Act I Scene 1, her open-mindedness towards the story of the lovers' adventures in the wood, and her fear that the craftsmen might be humiliated in their performance, mark her out as a woman who is thoughtful and kind, and also ready to defer to her husband's judgement when he responds to these concerns. In a play which contains such self-assertive women as Hermia, Titania and even (through Oberon's tribute to her as an 'imperial votress', II.1.163) Queen Elizabeth I, such passive behaviour seems surprising. Hippolyta is, after all, the Queen of the Amazons, leader of a nation of female warriors, and Titania characterises her with the vigorous word 'bouncing' (II.1.70).

HIPPOLYTA AS A SYMBOL OF PASSION

The answer may lie in the Elizabethans' traditional view of the Amazons as a **symbol** of passions needing to be governed by reason, just as women (so it was assumed) needed to be governed by men. This view of the Amazons is found, for example, in Edmund Spenser's poem *The Faerie Queene* (1596) and in *The Two Noble Kinsmen* (1613), a play of which Shakespeare is thought to be joint-author. The defeat of the Amazons by Theseus and the marriage of their queen, Hippolyta, to her conqueror may be intended as a reassurance that this play will not ultimately support emotional and/or female rebellion against society. As the action progresses, we see Oberon defeat Titania, and Hermia succeeds in defying her unjust father only through the intervention of two superior male authority figures, Oberon and Theseus, after which she apparently reverts to wifely obedience.

STUDY FOCUS: ACTING HIPPOLYTA · A04

If Hippolyta symbolises female deference and possibly also the subordination of emotion to reason, there still remains the basic problem of how she is to be played as an individual character. Her long silences and her slight disagreements with Theseus when she does speak may indicate some animosity between the two of them. In Act I Scene 1 she implies that she is in no hurry for their wedding night. In Act IV Scene 1 she responds coolly to Theseus's praise of his hunting dogs by praising someone else's. In Act V Scene 1 she questions Theseus's interpretation of the lovers' stories and is generally unappreciative of the play he has chosen for their entertainment. While it is possible for an actress to play Hippolyta as a doting fiancée and wife, the text accommodates a tenser relationship and in some productions she has successfully been presented as an unwilling captive, resentful of a military defeat and a diplomatic marriage.

CONTEXT · A04

In a version staged in San Francisco in 1966, Hippolyta made her first entry as a caged prisoner, making it clear that she was marrying against her will. Do you think that this is an effective way of staging the opening scene?

KEY QUOTATION: HIPPOLYTA · A01

Looking ahead to her marriage, Hippolyta says that: 'Four days will quickly steep themselves in night; / Four nights will quickly dream away the time' (I.1.7–8).

Possible interpretations:

● Hippolyta is not nearly as impatient for the wedding night as Theseus.
● Perhaps she does not really want to marry him at all.

EGEUS

WHO IS EGEUS?

- Egeus is Hermia's father, who is determined to marry her to Demetrius.
- He even asks Theseus to have his daughter executed if she disobeys his will.

EGEUS AS A PLOT DEVICE

Egeus is a **stock character** of **comedy**, the self-righteous father determined to thwart his daughter's choice of husband. In most editions and performances he appears in the play only twice, once in the opening scene to threaten Hermia with execution if she does not marry Demetrius, then again in Act IV Scene 1 to accept Theseus's ruling that she can marry Lysander after all. The contrast between the sustained complaining of his first appearance and the way he rapidly gives in on his second appearance may seem surprising, but it happens because he is a merely functional character, included in the play not for his interesting personality and behaviour but to advance the story. If the actor who plays him avoids drawing attention to himself when he is not speaking, we will not give Egeus much thought and so will not feel a sense of contradiction in his behaviour. Alternatively, recalling that Theseus has given Egeus 'some private schooling' (I.1.116) between his two appearances – presumably criticising his unreasonable treatment of Hermia – we can imagine a performance where Theseus's line, 'Egeus, I will overbear your will' (IV.1.176) is delivered in such a forceful manner that no Athenian citizen would dare to contradict it. The actor playing Egeus could then behave in a comically deflated or touchingly sad manner, according to preference.

STUDY FOCUS: EGEUS'S THIRD APPEARANCE A04

In the earliest version of *A Midsummer Night's Dream* to be published, in the text we now refer to as the First Quarto, Philostrate appears at the start of Act V to tell Theseus about the entertainments on offer for his wedding celebrations. In the later First Folio version, however, he is replaced by Egeus and Lysander. Presumably the change was made in order to cut the small role of Philostrate out of the play. This reappearance by Egeus gives him another chance to show his feelings. By speaking politely to Theseus and Lysander, he can demonstrate that he has been reconciled to Hermia's choice of husband, or by speaking his lines with wounded dignity he can suggest the opposite. Barbara Hodgdon has pointed out that Egeus's feelings will inevitably be revealed by his actions when he leaves the stage. Does he depart sadly on his own, does he angrily turn his back on his daughter and fall in behind Theseus and Hippolyta, or does he instead accompany Hermia and Lysander, perhaps offering them a hug and a handshake as the three depart?

CRITICAL VIEWPOINT A03

Barbara Hodgdon suggests that Egeus's appearance in Act V of the First Folio is an example of Shakespeare revising and improving his playscript, creating a greater sense of 'familial and community harmony'. However, most productions stick with the First Quarto and give his lines to Philostrate. Which approach do you prefer?

KEY QUOTATION: EGEUS A01

'As she is mine I may dispose of her; / Which shall be either to this gentleman / Or to her death' (I.1.42–4).

Possible interpretations:

- Egeus treats his daughter as a possession, not a person with feelings and opinions.
- He is so angry at her defiance that he is prepared to threaten her with execution.
- His exaggerated threats show him to be a fool and, while we may feel sorry for Hermia, we have little doubt that she will defeat him in the end.

HERMIA

WHO IS HERMIA?

- Hermia is Egeus's daughter.
- She is threatened with death or imprisonment in a convent unless she marries her father's choice of husband, Demetrius.
- Instead she elopes with her preferred suitor, Lysander.

HERMIA'S APPEARANCE

Hermia is the darker and shorter of the two young women. 'Who will not change a raven for a dove?' asks Lysander (II.2.120), contrasting her complexion and hair colour with Helena's. Later he calls Hermia an 'Ethiope' and a 'tawny Tartar' (III.2.257 and 263), a 'dwarf', a 'bead' and an 'acorn' (III.2.328–30). Dark hair and skin were considered unfashionable in this period, but before the magic juice distorts their reactions both men still perceive Hermia as highly attractive.

STUDY FOCUS: HERMIA'S PERSONALITY A02

It may be her unfashionable appearance that has encouraged Hermia to be self-assertive, or perhaps she just takes after her father Egeus, who does not seem bashful in expressing his opinions. In the first scene she is prepared to defy not only her father but Duke Theseus. Although she inserts the maidenly disclaimer, 'I know not by what power I am made bold' (I.1.59), she has plenty of reserves of courage left shortly afterwards to agree to elope with Lysander. On her arrival in the forest, she firmly insists that Lysander sleeps separately from her. When she thinks Demetrius may have killed Lysander she becomes highly aggressive ('Out, dog! Out, cur!', III.2.65) and when she thinks that Helena has stolen Lysander's love she threatens her with violence ('my nails can reach unto thine eyes', III.2.298). She is rather mercurial (active and changeable) in temperament, and her name appropriately enough seems to derive from that of Hermes, the ever-moving messenger of the Greek gods, known to the Romans as Mercury.

KEY QUOTATION: HERMIA A01

Hermia says she would rather suffer punishment than marry Demetrius to 'whose unwished yoke / My soul consents not to give sovereignty' (I.1.81–2).

Possible interpretations:

- Hermia has too much self-respect to marry a man chosen for her by her father and is not afraid to say so.
- She feels she is being treated like an animal, yoked to a plough without choice.
- She wants to marry Lysander whom she loves.

Other useful quotations:

Helena's assessment of her: 'though she be but little, she is fierce' (III.2.325).

Hermia's confusion at the end of the night: 'Methinks I see these things with parted eye, / When everything seems double' (IV.1.186–7).

CONTEXT A02

The lovers use the standard language of Elizabethan love poetry, featuring exaggerated comparisons of the beloved to objects in nature, mythology and religion, except when they quarrel and drop into a lower **register** of abusiveness. These sudden shift from compliments to insults are so extreme and ridiculous that they guarantee laughter from the audience.

CRITICAL VIEWPOINT A03

Hermia seems a resilient character, but Norman Holland argues that her dream of being attacked by a snake while Lysander watches (II.2.151–62) shows her inner vulnerability. The snake is a **symbol** of loveless desire, triggering a fear of betrayal in us all. Do you agree that her nightmare adds emotional depth to the play?

HELENA

WHO IS HELENA?

- Helena has been rejected by Demetrius, but she still loves him.
- She continues to pursue Demetrius, even to the extent of letting herself be humiliated.
- By the time that the magic juice causes both Demetrius and Lysander to reject Hermia and fall in love with Helena, she has lost so much self-esteem that she does not believe it when they tell her how attractive she is.

HELENA THE VICTIM

Helena's name means Light, fittingly as she is fair in colouring, as well as tall. She seems at first to be confident of her own attractiveness ('Through Athens I am thought as fair as she', I.1.227), but having been rejected by Demetrius before the play begins, she has less self-esteem than Hermia and is comparatively timid. Her betrayal of the elopement plans to Demetrius, her undignified pursuit of him to the wood, her inability to credit that Demetrius and Lysander have fallen in love with her, and finally her lengthy appeal to Hermia to respect their childhood friendship, culminating in a call for 'pity' and an absurd forecast of her own 'death' (III.2.235 and 244), are all the actions of someone who has come to see herself as a victim. Her final lines express wonderment that she has been reunited with Demetrius, coupled with a lingering uncertainty. After all that she has been through, part of her feels he is still 'not mine own' (IV.1.189).

STUDY FOCUS: SILENT WOMEN   A02

There are several interesting moments in *A Midsummer Night's Dream* brought about by what is not said. The silences force us to read between the lines in order to get at the characters' possible reactions. In Act I Scene 1, Hippolyta makes no comment on the forced marriage with which Hermia is threatened. The actors and the audience, or the readers of the play, have to put themselves in her place and imagine how she might feel. Similarly, Helena and Hermia are on stage for most of Act V, but neither of them speaks. We do not know how they act towards their husbands or their elders or how they respond to the performance of 'Pyramus and Thisbe'. Some critics have speculated that they are still in shock at their treatment in the wood, but it may simply be that they are no longer so significant to the story once they are married and that it would not be proper for young wives to join in the banter over the play.

KEY QUOTATION: HELENA   A01

'Use me but as your spaniel: spurn me, strike me, / Neglect me, lose me; only give me leave, / Unworthy as I am, to follow you' (II.1.205–7).

Possible interpretations:

- Helena will endure any treatment from Demetrius, so long as he notices her.
- Helena may even be getting some kind of pleasure out of her humiliation.
- Helena is someone who likes to exaggerate her feelings for effect.

Other useful quotations:

Demetrius started the relationship: he 'made love to Nedar's daughter, Helena' (I.1.107).

Demetrius reappraises her under the spell: 'O Helen, goddess, nymph, perfect, divine!' (III.2.137).

Helena admits her own folly: 'You see how simple and how fond I am' (III.2.317).

CONTEXT   A04

We feel sorry for Helena, but her self-pity is also a source of comedy. In a production directed by Kenneth Branagh in 1990, Emma Thompson as Helena swooned melodramatically in Act III Scene 2 when she spoke of escaping further misery through her death, then suddenly jerked backed upright with a second thought and added 'or absence' (line 244).

DEMETRIUS

WHO IS DEMETRIUS?

- Demetrius is a young aristocrat who once loved Helena.
- He wants to marry Hermia and has her father's consent for the match, but not Hermia's.
- Alterted by Helena, he goes to the wood to stop Hermia eloping with Lysander.
- Robin eventually uses the magic juice to restore his love for Helena.

DEMETRIUS: THE LEAST LIKEABLE OF THE LOVERS

Demetrius is a less sympathetic figure than Lysander. Before the play begins he has courted Helena, then abandoned her for Hermia. He remains determined to marry Hermia, regardless of the fact that she is in love with someone else. If he was actually 'betrothed' to Helena, as he seems to admit at IV.1.169, then it is doubtful whether a marriage to Hermia would have been legal. In Act I Scene 1 he has little to say and we see him ridiculed by Lysander. In Act II Scene 1 he is comically pursued around the stage by Helena. In Act III Scene 2 he is unpleasant to Hermia when she is distraught at the loss of Lysander. Only when the magic juice has been placed on his eyes does he show honour and dignity, and in fact he is the only one of the four lovers from whom the spell is never removed. This has worried some critics, who feel that his love for Helena is consequently a false one and that this inauthenticity detracts from the happy ending. In response, however, it has been argued that Demetrius has only been restored to his original love, the 'natural taste' of which he speaks so movingly when he awakens in the morning (IV.1.171).

CONTEXT · A04

Demetrius says he was 'betrothed' to Helena (IV.1.169). A betrothal was an engagement ceremony in which the man gave the woman a ring and the couple signed an agreement about the financial arrangements. Shakespeare himself would help arrange a betrothal in 1604 and be summoned to court in 1612 to testify on the details of the dowry.

STUDY FOCUS: GENDER · A02

The two young women remain constant in their allegiance throughout the play; it is the men whose attachments change. Despite the affection which Hermia and Helena feel for them, the two male lovers never display any originality or insight, finishing the play by making derisive comments about 'Pyramus and Thisbe', quite unable to detect its relevance to their own experience.

The idea that women are more 'constant' than men occurs elsewhere in Shakespeare's comedies. In *Twelfth Night*, for example, Viola takes advantage of her disguise as a boy to challenge Duke Orsino's sexism and proclaim to him that women are more 'true of heart'. How do you view the lovers in the play?

CONTEXT · A04

Nineteenth-century directors found the lovers' quarrels in Act III Scene 2 over-long and cut many of their lines. Twentieth-century directors have retained the lines, but livened up their delivery with lots of physical comedy. In one 1981 production Demetrius was knocked down by Hermia, who then trod on his hand and pulled his hair. Do you think the scene benefits from this kind of action?

KEY QUOTATION: DEMETRIUS · A01

To Helena: 'I love thee not, therefore pursue me not' (II.1.188).

Possible interpretations:

- Demetrius no longer loves Helena and bluntly expresses his wishes to be rid of her.
- Demetrius is trying to deny his love for Helena, but she knows that deep down he still loves her.
- Demetrius does not love Helena, but her love is so strong that she will overcome him regardless.

LYSANDER

WHO IS LYSANDER?

- Lysander loves Hermia, but is turned down by her father, Egeus.
- He elopes with Hermia, but they become lost in the wood.
- The magic juice makes him fall temporarily in love with Helena.

LYSANDER'S STRENGTHS

Lysander is for the most part a model young aristocrat. He has wooed Hermia with poems, songs and gifts. He is coolly assertive in his dealings with Egeus and Demetrius, putting down his rival with the retort, 'You have her father's love … Do you marry him' (I.1.94). He is smoothly courteous to Theseus, keeping his temper and arguing his case logically. This evidently makes a good impression on the Duke because in the Folio version of Act V he is allowed to assist Theseus by reading the descriptions of the proposed entertainments. His elopement plan, to run off to his wealthy aunt's home and marry Hermia beyond the reach of the Athenian law, shows initiative, though his inability to find his way through the wood takes away some of our admiration for him.

STUDY FOCUS: LYSANDER UNDER THE SPELL `A03`

The attitudes of Lysander and Hermia diverge a little when he tries to sleep with her in the wood and she has to instruct him to move further away. Under the influence of the magic juice, however, their relationship comes decisively to an end. Lysander first abandons Hermia, then becomes extremely abusive to her and threatens to kill Demetrius. This is shockingly out of line with his earlier behaviour. Some critics think that we are seeing the repressed lust and anger that lay beneath Lysander's civilised surface all along and that the humiliation inflicted on the women here is a signficiant part of the story, leaving a sour aftertaste to the comedy. However, the sudden change of the men's speech from loving compliments to extravagant insults, together with the women's switch from friendship to mutual recrimination, seems likelier to amuse and entertain an audience, rather than shock them. Is our view of Lysander and the others changed by their behaviour under the spell of the magic juice, or do we view it as an amusing interlude which can later be disregarded?

CHECK THE FILM `A03`

In most film and stage productions Lysander and Demetrius seem almost interchangeable. The 1935 film makes a greater effort than most to differentiate between them, showing an arrogant Demetrius and a Lysander who mocks him with a comical swagger and cheeky face-pulling.

KEY QUOTATION: LYSANDER `A01`

Lysander defends abandoning Hermia for Helena: 'The will of man is by his reason swayed / And reason says you are the worthier maid' (II.2.121–2).

Possible interpretations:

- Lysander believes he is acting rationally.
- He is not acting rationally as he is under the spell of the magic juice.
- Love has more to do with instinct and emotion than it has with rational choice.

REVISION FOCUS: TASK 4 `A03`

How far do you agree with the statements below?

- There is little to choose between Lysander and Demetrius.
- The speeches of the lovers have often been drastically cut and rightly so.

Try writing opening paragraphs for essays based on these discussion points. Set out your arguments clearly.

BOTTOM

WHO IS BOTTOM?

- Bottom, a weaver, is the leading actor in the craftsmen's play.
- During rehearsal the puck puts him under a spell and gives him the head of an ass.
- Titania the fairy queen, also under a spell, falls in love with him.
- Freed from the spell, Bottom successfully acts the part of Pyramus in the play to celebrate the weddings.

BOTTOM'S NAME

The craftsmen's names reflect their jobs (see **Part Two: Act I Scene 2**), but Bottom's name may not only refer to the bottom (reel) from which a weaver unwinds his thread. It may also carry the sense of 'bottom' as 'the sitting part of the body', which ties in neatly with his later transformation into an 'ass'. Some scholars find this idea unacceptably vulgar, but Shakespeare does seem to use the word 'ass' this way in *Hamlet* Act II Scene 2.

BOTTOM'S CHARACTER

Nick Bottom is called by the puck 'the shallowest thickskin of that barren sort' (III.2.13), but he is always full of ideas and enthusiasm, and it is his bumptious self-confidence as much as Quince's powers of organisation which carries the play through rehearsals and performance. Without him, the others simply give up. They call him 'Bully', a friendly and appreciative term (III.1.7 and IV.2.15). He shares something of the exuberance of the puck and, like him, aspires to take on different identities (a woman, a lion and, best of all, a ranting, swaggering tyrant). Whereas the puck is able to call upon supernatural powers to become a foal, a stool and so on, Bottom has to be content with what can be done by mere acting – at least until the puck lends him a hand with his magic spells. Fortunately, Bottom is too thick-skinned to notice how bad an actor he is. This insensitivity proves to be his salvation. Even when equipped with an ass's head and propositioned by the queen of the fairies, he is not seriously alarmed or even curious about what has happened to him, but gets on with playing with relish the part in which he finds himself. In his dealings with the fairies, he is not at all self-conscious about mimicking courtly speech and manners. Indeed he manages to be considerably more civilised than the real aristocrats who jeer at his play in Act V. Since it is likely that the fairies would have originally been played by children, his kindly, slightly patronising treatment of them would probably have been seen in a positive light by the audience.

CONTEXT **A04**

The Lord Chamberlain's Men was a leading theatrical company from 1594 to 1603, with Shakespeare as their chief dramatist and Richard Burbage as their chief actor. Their patron, the Lord Chamberlain, was in charge of entertainment at court, where they often performed. When King James I succeeded Elizabeth, they were renamed the King's Men and continued performing until the closure of the theatres in 1642.

STUDY FOCUS: BOTTOM AS A HERO **A02**

When restored to his normal self, Bottom struggles to find words for his bizarre experiences, but is not overcome by them and is soon enthusing his fellow craftsmen and acting his heart out. When his courtly audience mock him, he gives as good as he gets and wins them over. The actor who first played Bottom was probably Will Kempe, who was the star clown of Shakespeare's company. Kempe was famous for his dancing (after he left the Lord Chamberlain's Men, he kept his name before the public by dancing from London to Norwich), so when in Act V the craftsmen perform a bergomask dance, we have to picture a high-powered, expertly comical display which would have brought Bottom's performance to an end on a very high note. Although we laugh at Bottom for his crude acting, insensitive self-assertion and lack of polish, we also laugh with him because of his adaptability and his determination to keep going and succeed when a 'wiser' man would have given up.

KEY QUOTATION: BOTTOM   A01

Upon awaking after his adventures, Bottom says: 'The eye of man hath not heard, the ear of man hath not seen, man's hand is not able to taste, his tongue to conceive, nor his heart to report what my dream was!' (IV.1205–7).

Possible interpretations:

- Bottom is confused and only half awake, so mangles his words.
- Bottom has experienced something so strange that it is beyond description.
- The echoes of the Bible (1 Corinthians 2. 9–10) suggest that Bottom may have achieved an insight beyond reason and worldly wisdom.

Other useful quotations:

Bottom's wisdom: 'Nay, I can gleek upon occasion' (III.1.122).

Bottom's intelligence and presence, praised by Francis Flute: 'he hath simply the best wit of any handicraft man in Athens … and the best person, too' (IV.2.7–8).

THE CRAFTSMEN

The craftsmen are described patronisingly by others (to Robin they are 'hempen homespuns', III.1.60, to Philostrate 'Hard-handed men … Which never laboured in their minds till now', V.1.72–3). When they try to use a wide vocabulary they mix up their words and their attempts to write and stage a **tragedy** are highly comical, all in a way calculated to amuse regular theatregoers and the well-educated. Nonetheless, we enjoy their struggle with the demands of drama and we admire their determination to succeed.

Most of the craftsmen receive little individual character development. We know that Francis Flute the bellows-mender is the youngest, his voice unbroken, his beard still 'coming' (I.2.39) and for these reasons he is assigned the role of Thisbe. Snug the joiner is 'slow of study' (I.2.55) so is made the lion, a role with no (or, as it turns out, just a few) lines. Tom Snout the tinker is originally cast as Thisbe's father, then switched to the somewhat limited role of a wall. Similarly, Robin Starveling the tailor is changed from playing Thisbe's mother to Moonshine, where he is put off by heckling and fails to deliver all of his speech. All four men look for guidance to Peter Quince the carpenter, who seems to be not only the director, but also the author of 'Pyramus and Thisbe'. Since there is no record of classical plays being acted by workers, Quince is certainly original in his ideas and he behaves throughout as the leader of the project, assigning the parts, taking on the rewriting, directing the rehearsals and, not least among his achievements, flattering Bottom into co-operation. His speech is always decisive in tone, until he is before the audience at the palace, where he suffers a loss of nerve and delivers his lines badly in the role of Prologue.

Since the 1960s some performances of the play have been influenced by Jan Kott's claim that it is 'erotic' and that the addition of an ass head turns Bottom into a sexual fantasy figure. The 1981 BBC version teases the audience by showing Bottom atop Titania making suggestive noises which in the end lead only to a sneeze.

CRITICAL VIEWPOINT A03

The social significance of Quince's troupe is a matter of dispute. To Peter Hollindale the 'mechanicals' endorse the social system through their 'safe and certain knowledge' of their place in society To Elliot Krieger the 'craftsmen' are exploited workers who find themselves 'incorporated into the ruling-class vision of society'. To Kiernan Ryan they are natural subversives who upstage and **parody** the aristocrats. What do you think?

OBERON

WHO IS OBERON?

- Oberon is the king of the fairies.
- He quarrels with the queen, Titania, and plays a trick on her, using magic juice to make her fall in love with the first creature that she sees.
- Wishing to help the mortal lovers, he sends Robin the puck to resolve their conflicts with the magic juice, and succeeds on the third attempt.

OBERON THE FAIRY KING

Oberon has natural authority. His speech is always decisive. He constantly issues orders and is used to getting his way. He may strike a modern audience, attuned to ideals of democracy and equality, as a slightly sinister figure. Both the puck and Titania call him 'jealous Oberon' (II.1.24 and 61). In particular, we may suspect his motives in wanting the little boy. However, it can be argued that Titania is holding back the child from his natural growth into manhood, crowning him with flowers when he should be taking on the masculine role of knight.

STUDY FOCUS: THE TWO SIDES OF OBERON   A03

Like other key elements of the play, the character of Oberon has two sides to it; we see first one, then the other. He is swift in his mood changes, fiercely jealous, but then forgiving and helpful. However, he is not human, but a mythical figure, embodying Elizabethan ideas of masculinity. He does make a consistent effort to help Helena and the others, taking pity on her as 'a sweet Athenian lady' (II.1.260) and three times sending Robin to intervene until she finally gets her love. Oberon has supernatural powers, being able to see further into the heavens than Robin, understand the power of the magic juice, and in the last scene cast a protective spell over unborn children. In his speeches he is capable of a descriptive beauty beyond that achieved by the mortal characters.

KEY QUOTATION: OBERON   A01

Oberon replies to the puck's description of ghosts who haunt by night: 'But we are spirits of another sort. / I with the morning's love have oft made sport' (III.2.388–9).

Possible interpretations:

- Oberon and the fairies are not evil spirits, so they are not afraid of light and are able to continue their activities into the twilight.
- Oberon has a mystical relationship with the goddess of the dawn.
- Oberon can even play or hunt during daylight with the blessing of this goddess.

Other useful quotations:

Putting a spell on his wife: 'I'll streak her eyes / And make her full of hateful fantasies' (II.1.257–8).

Blessing the lovers: 'back to Athens shall the lovers wend / With league whose date till death shall never end' (III.2.372–3).

CHECK THE FILM   A03

In the nineteenth century Oberon was usually played by a woman, which made him seem ethereal and otherworldly. More recently, the emphasis has been on his exotic but masculine authority. In Michael Hoffman's 1999 film, for example, he resembles a handsome Greek god, in the 1981 BBC production a long-haired chieftian.

TITANIA

WHO IS TITANIA?

- Titania is the queen of the fairies.
- She has fallen out with the king, Oberon, over an Indian boy.
- Because Oberon orders magic juice to be put on her eyes in revenge, she falls in love with Bottom who, in a further prank by the puck, has been given the head of an ass.

TITANIA, THE QUEEN OF THE FAIRIES

Titania is like Oberon in many respects. She, too, is authoritative, well-intentioned towards the mortals and capable of speaking in memorably poetic lines. Although she is seen to be caring and maternal in her attitude towards her votress and 'young squire' (II.1.131), and towards the human beings harmed by the unseasonable weather, under the influence of the magic juice she does show a more possessive side to her nature, caring for Bottom but also taking him prisoner with the words, 'Thou shalt remain here, whether thou wilt or no' (III.1.127).

STUDY FOCUS: TITANIA THE GODDESS OF NATURE `A03`

Shakespeare seems to assume that, as an embodiment of natural femininity, Titania must inevitably submit to her husband's will in the end. However, she is by no means easily dominated. Her name seems to have come from Ovid's *Metamorphoses*, where it is a synonym for a goddess, Diana. She firmly defies Oberon, answering him back and targetting him with a series of accusations, until he resorts to drugging her with the magic juice. According to Regina Buccola, folklore presents Titania as the real ruler of the fairies. Oberon is referred to in only a few folktales and then as her consort, not her equal. In this reading of the play, Titania and Theseus are both legitimate rulers, and Oberon is a subversive figure who undermines the decisions of both of them.

CRITICAL VIEWPOINT `A03`

Several critics have argued that Titania represents the fear of female authority felt by many men in Shakespeare's day, not least because they lived under the rule of the formidable queen Elizabeth. This view is put especially clearly by Helen Hackett in chapter 2 of her study, *A Midsummer Night's Dream* (1997).

KEY QUOTATION: TITANIA `A01`

Titania introduces herself to Bottom: 'I am a spirit of no common rate; / The summer still doth tend upon my state' (III.1.128–9).

Possible interpretations

- Titania is one of the most powerful and important spirits.
- The summer obeys Titania and follows her movements.
- Titania can easily abduct Bottom and make her follow him too.

Other useful quotations:

Titania blames herself and Oberon for the weather events: 'We are their parents and original' (II.1.117).

Titania loved the mother of the Indian boy: 'for her sake do I rear up her boy; / And for her sake I will not part with him' (II.1136–7).

THE PUCK

WHO IS THE PUCK?

- The puck Robin Goodfellow is a type of goblin, who entertains and assists Oberon the fairy king.
- He enjoys practical jokes, including terrifying the craftsmen by giving Bottom the head of an ass. Oberon ensures that the puck does not do anyone any lasting harm.

THE PUCK AS A GOBLIN

Shakespeare sets him down in the original stage directions as 'Robin', 'Rob' or 'Puck'. Most editions of the play have adopted 'Puck' as a general title for him, but that is not his name. His name is Robin and he is *a* puck, a kind of goblin, as he himself observes (III.2.399). He is not a fairy; the fairy in Act II Scene 1 certainly recognises him as different from herself. Before Shakespeare, he was not classified as a puck either, but as an earth spirit. In folklore he always carried a broom with him (as he does in Act V, when he tells us 'I am sent with broom before', V.1.367) so that he could help maids who had behaved well and so deserved his assistance. He also took a great interest in sorting out love conflicts, as in a fashion he does in *A Midsummer Night's Dream*. His last name, Goodfellow, was added by countryfolk who wished to flatter him into leaving them alone.

CRITICAL VIEWPOINT A03

In his essay 'But We Are Spirits of Another Sort' (1975), David Bevington suggests that the puck represents the sinister aspects of the fairy world. The audience may be amused by his presence, but the mortal characters are terrified as he turns their fears against them, creating 'truly frightening illusions in the forest'. The exception is Bottom who, as the puck complains, is too much of a 'thick-skin' to be vulnerable to him (III.2.13).

STUDY FOCUS: THE PUCK AS A THEATRICAL DEVICE A03

The puck delights in mischief and so his presence on stage is enjoyed by the audience as one who brings them fun, which he does without offending our conscience and our sense of identification with the victims. With one exception (the fairy in Act II Scene 1), he speaks only to Oberon and the audience, with the result that he seems almost to exist outside the rest of the drama, unconstrained by the actions and expectations of others.

THE PUCK'S VERSATILITY

The puck is free to use a wide range of **verse** forms, **couplets** of various lengths and **quatrains** as well as **blank verse**, and he employs a wide range of tones. Where Bottom aspires to play the hero, the love interest and the lion, the puck can actually become a foal, a crab, a stool, a horse, a dog, a hog, a bear and even a fire, but to a still greater degree than Bottom he is unaffected by his experiences and always remains himself. While the marriages change the mortals who undertake them as a pivotal part of their journey through life to death, the spirits are immortal, immaterial and so incapable of development.

CRITICAL VIEWPOINT A03

To some extent, the puck is our representative, carrying out the mischief we hope to enjoy, commenting on it and addressing us directly at the end.

KEY QUOTATION: THE PUCK A01

The puck enters the palace: 'I am sent with broom before / To sweep the dust behind the door' (V.1.367–8).

Possible interpretations:

- The puck's sweeping up shows that, despite his pranks, he is a friend to human beings.
- The fact that he is 'sent' shows that he remains under the control of Oberon, who is keeps his mischief within bounds.

Other useful quotations:

The puck's occupation: 'I am that merry wanderer of the night. / I jest to Oberon, and make him smile' (II.1.43–4).

His enjoyment: 'those things do best please me / That befall prepost'rously' (III.2.120–1).

THE FAIRIES

Traditionally, fairies had been conceived of as much more hostile figures than they are in *A Midsummer Night's Dream*. Even in Shakespeare's other plays they are mentioned as creatures which torment mortals by pinching them. Here they are comparatively well-meaning, though not as sweet and flimsy as they were to become in later literature. It is made clear that they are not from the underworld, as Christians who believed in their existence but rejected pagan superstition would logically assume, but 'spirits of another sort' (III.2.388).

Their references to India and to their speedy globetrotting convey a sense of freedom and power. Unlike the fairies of tradition, they perform neighbourly deeds without demanding payment. They do not abduct children, but instead quarrel over who is to adopt and care for the little orphan boy. Their only venture into kidnapping and bewitching is the transformation of Bottom, who is fed, flattered and restored unharmed, without having a limb lopped off or his sanity destroyed as was the traditional fairy practice. Far from deliberately hurting people, they show guilt about their influence on the weather and eagerly bless the triple wedding. Such wicked fairy deeds as are mentioned in the play are attributed to the puck alone, who is not an evil spirit, merely 'shrewd and knavish' (II.1.33), and is kept on a tight rein by the king, Oberon, who uses him as a combined jester and assistant.

STUDY FOCUS: CASTING THE FAIRIES `A04`

Titania, Oberon and the puck seem to be the same size as humans – Titania is able to take Bottom in her arms. These three otherworldy figures are sometimes played by the same actors as Hippolyta, Theseus and Philostrate, suggesting that they express the mortals' dream selves. Their attendants, who are able to hide inside flowers and fight bees, are much smaller and are sometimes played by child actors – though if and when children are not available, the actors playing Snout, Snug, Flute and Starveling can conveniently double the parts.

The fairies embody the forces of nature. Titania's four attendants are named after natural medicines (see **Part Two: Act III Scene 1**). The effect of this **personification** is to make the world seem a place which, though it may be unpredictable and sometimes dangerous, is ultimately friendly to the human species, even similar in its structure to Elizabethan society. However, like all elements of the play, there is a reverse side to this conception. The audience never forgets that the world of the fairies is a comic device. We enjoy seeing a 'humanised' version of nature, but we know that the real world of nature is not like this.

THEMES

LOVE

A SOURCE OF COMEDY

Traditionally, a **comedy** is a play about two lovers whose path to marriage is blocked by members of the older generation. After a series of entertaining **plot** devices, they succeed in getting the upper hand and marrying after all. In his earlier comedies Shakespeare had shown a liking for making the traditional comic situations still more farcical by bringing on to the stage not simply two lovers but two or more pairs of them, and even making some of them identical twins (*The Comedy of Errors* features two pairs of identical twins, both named Antipholus and Dromio). One objection to this approach is that to place so much emphasis on elaborate plot development can make the portrayal of love shallow and unconvincing. Towards the end of *The Two Gentlemen of Verona*, for example, Valentine decides to make a gift of the woman he loves, Silvia, to his old friend Proteus, even though Proteus has tried to rape her a few moments before. This provides an interesting twist to the plot, but in doing so damages the **characterisation** beyond repair. In *A Midsummer Night's Dream*, however, Shakespeare converts the potential defect into an advantage. He puts the irrationality of love at the very centre of the play and makes it one of its chief subjects.

POTENTIAL FOR TRAGEDY

The basic comic plot of a father (Egeus) attempting to thwart a young couple (Hermia and Lysander) is developed in comparatively routine fashion, so much so that its resolution is accomplished in one line: 'Egeus, I will overbear your will' (IV.1.176). However, the love plot is such an accepted theatrical device and so powerful in its appeal, that it survives this, just as it survives the introduction of a second couple, Helena and Demetrius (still more couples, if we also count Theseus and Hippolyta and Oberon and Titania). The acts of courtship between Lysander and Hermia which Egeus dismisses as 'feigning' (I.1.31) are accepted by the audience as signs of emotional commitment, and we are moved by the couple's willingness to die rather than live parted. Hermia, in particular, is ready to risk execution or a lifetime imprisoned in a convent. Both partners are aware that lovers before them have come to sad ends, and the story of Pyramus and Thisbe, however ineptly executed by the craftsmen, reminds us that love can be a source of **tragedy** as easily as of comedy. Its striking similarity to the story of Romeo and Juliet is a reminder that if Egeus had got his way, Lysander and Hermia might also have ended by killing themselves in despair.

CHECK THE PLAY **A03**

Shakespeare's *Romeo and Juliet* and *A Midsummer Night's Dream* were both written around 1596. Both plays depict a girl who tries to escape a forced marriage by eloping and both feature violent confrontation. It seems that they form a pair, telling similar stories with contrasting outcomes. It is therefore well worth seeing or reading *Romeo and Juliet* to see how similar material can be used for tragedy or comedy.

STUDY FOCUS: THE DISRUPTIVE NATURE OF LOVE A02

The love interest with which the play opens is soon modified by Helena's **soliloquy** at the end of Act I Scene 1, which highlights not so much the importance or danger of love as its subjective, irrational nature. In Acts II and III the intervention of Oberon and Robin with their magic juice speeds up the process of falling in and out of love in a way which makes it highly comical. The lovers' speeches, which try to explain and justify their love as rational, only serve to make their behaviour seem more absurd. As in Shakespeare's other plays and his **sonnets**, love is depicted as a kind of positive illness, which can exist in contradiction to one's normal feelings and ideas, and which can sometimes lead us to do things which are foolish or hurtful. Love's reverse side is jealousy. While the audience are joining in with Robin's laughter at the folly of the mortals, Lysander and Demetrius are trying to kill one another, and Helena and Hermia are suffering from the scornful rejection which they have received from the men whom they love.

THE LOVING COUPLES

In the end love is not denied. Hermia has her Lysander, Helena has her Demetrius, and, for that matter, Theseus has his Hippolyta, and Oberon his Titania – though, like the younger lovers, the two older couples experience serious difficulties along the way, Theseus and Hippolyta making war against each other before the play begins, and Oberon and Titania becoming temporarily estranged by their quarrel.

We must not forget the fifth couple, who make the oddest pairing of all. Titania and Bottom share the shortest time together, but it is long enough to demonstrate the extremes of love's irrationality. When Titania embraces Bottom, Shakespeare seems to be telling us that sexual attraction is not only arbitrary, but liable by its nature sometimes to take forms which are impractical or perverse. Shakespeare makes a similar point in his sonnets, written around this time, in which the poet, who finds himself fixated both upon a lady as unfashionably dark as Hermia and upon a man as disloyal as Demetrius, can only exclaim, 'O me! what eyes hath Love put in my head, / Which have no correspondence with true sight ... ?' (Sonnet 148).

KEY QUOTATION: LOVE A01

When Egeus asks Demetrius why he has ceased to love Hermia, he can only answer, 'all the faith, the virtue of my heart, / The object and the pleasure of mine eye, / Is only Helena' (IV.1.166–8).

Possible interpretations:

- Demetrius is so in love with Helena that she is the source of his happiness and the inspiration for all his good qualities.
- He cannot explain why he loves her, because love comes from emotion more than from reason.
- Demetrius still has the magic juice on his eyes. Does this make his love false?

CONTEXT A04

Shakespeare's most intensive reflections on love occur in his *Sonnets*, a book of poems published in 1609. It is not clear whether Shakespeare authorised their publication, to what degree they are autobiographical or whether the characters who appear in them can be identified with actual historical figures. The mysteries have only increased readers' fascination with the poems.

MARRIAGE

THE MARRIAGE OF OPPOSITES

Shakespeare was much influenced in this play by Ovid's *Metamorphoses*, a book of tales of supernatural transformation (see **Part Five: Literary background**). Unlike the changes portrayed by Ovid, however, the ones in *A Midsummer Night's Dream* are not always self-contained events. The changes which do fit that description are the short-term **plot** devices such as the ass's head and the magic juice. The major transformations – from rehearsal to performance, from child to adult, from single person to couple – each involve a growth from one state to the next and are more complex.

A Midsummer Night's Dream takes apparent oppositions and demonstrates either that they are natural stages in a process (youth and age, celibacy and sex, singleness and marriage) or that they are mutually supportive pairs (day and night, male and female, wakefulness and dreaming, actor and audience, city and wood, reason and imagination). Each side of these pairs has its own positive and negative aspects. The forest is both threatening and supportive; celibacy is both 'blessèd' and a 'withering' of life (I.1.74–7); Bottom is both an idiot and a hero; Theseus is both a wise ruler and a man of limited imagination.

WEDDINGS

The play does not suggest that one phenomenon or point of view is right and its opposite wrong, but seeks to marry them together to create something greater than either. In the case of eight of the characters it does so literally by marriage. *A Midsummer Night's Dream* is thematically a marriage play, whether or not it was written to celebrate a particular wedding. Marriage takes what might seem opposites – two people with separate experiences and aspirations – and reveals them to be potentially complementary to each other, creating something greater than the two were separately.

DIVINE HARMONY

Like humans, the elements can be in harmony or at odds, and the presence of Oberon and Titania implies that love between people is equivalent to, or an actual form of, the divine force which powers the world. Love, as we still say, makes the world go round. By setting his play in ancient Athens, Shakespeare avoids any awkward reference to religion, but the whole apparatus of the fairy world is a substitute for the mythologies and religions which human beings have devised to make sense of the world they inhabit.

STUDY FOCUS: MAY DAY A04

Appropriately, given its preoccupation with marriage and the movement from generation to generation, the play is shaped by the fertility rituals of Maying. May Day, when the countryside moves from spring to summer, was a time when people's thoughts turned to the fertility of the land and of their own species. Countryfolk danced round the phallic **symbol** of the 'painted maypole' (to which Hermia insultingly compares Helena at III.2.296). They went out into woods and hills while it was still night to have fun together and bring home branches for festive decoration, as Lysander reminds Hermia that they had once done with Helena (I.1.166–7). Such excursions provided an ideal opportunity for the young people to choose partners without the intervention of their elders and, as horrified Puritans pointed out, to engage in pre-marital sex. Scholars have argued that historically all comedy has its roots in fertility ceremonies, and *A Midsummer Night's Dream* certainly supports the case. Like candidates for a coming-of-age rite, the four lovers leave the city and their rationally ordered, comprehensible daytime world and, entering the wood, pass through a night of irrational, dream-like experiences which transforms them from disobedient children into adults accepted by society and partnered in marriage, ready now to become parents themselves.

CONTEXT A04

Even today May Day is celebrated in many parts of Britain. Padstow, Cornwall, is famous for its hobby horse parades and its singing; hobby horses also parade through the streets of Minehead, Somerset. In Oxford, a choir sings atop the tower of Magdalen Chapel. Many villages host dancing around a maypole, Ickwell in Bedfordshire boasting a red and white striped maypole seventy feet in height.

CITY AND COUNTRY

The shift of location between city and country is a favourite device in Shakespeare's comedies. A similar movement from the normal world to a **pastoral** one and back again also occurs in *The Two Gentlemen of Verona* and *As You Like It*, and there are comparable excursions in other plays like *The Merchant of Venice* and *The Winter's Tale*. In this case, the play begins and ends in Athens, a city famous for the reasoning powers of its great thinkers, Socrates, Plato and Aristotle; then, in total contrast, the long central section of the play spanning Acts II to IV, takes us to a wood outside the city's bounds, where human laws and reasoning virtually cease to apply. The rational, man-made world which rules the day and the non-rational, spontaneous world of dreams are both part of our experience; both are required when we pass through the great turning points and crises of our lives; both are involved in the creation of art.

KEY QUOTATION: MARRIAGE A01

Theseus tells Hippolyta, 'I wooed thee with my sword, / And won thy love doing thee injuries; / But I will wed thee in another key, / With pomp, with triumph, and with revelling' (I.1.16–19).

Possible interpretations:

- Marriage promises peace and reconciliation.
- Despite Theseus's fine words, his defeat of Hippolyta suggests that he still intends to be in charge in the marriage.
- His positive view of marriage is not supported by the behaviour of the only married couple we meet in the play, the wildly argumentative Oberon and Titania.

REVISION FOCUS: TASK 5 A03

How far do you agree with the statements below?

- The play ridicules marriage, implying that magic is needed to make it work.
- Beneath the comedy, the play offers a bleak view of love's irrationality.

Try writing opening paragraphs for essays based on these discussion points. Set out your arguments clearly.

GENDER

WOMEN AS ANIMALS?

The transformations in the play which have attracted most attention in recent years have been those connected with gender. To some degree the play seems to be an assertion of male authority. Robin Goodfellow intends to reassure us when he says:

> Jack shall have Jill;
> Naught shall go ill.
> The man shall have his mare again, and all shall be well. (III.2.461–3)

Today, however, to speak of woman in the same breath as animal property is more likely to give offence than reassurance. Worse still, the playwright puts similar sentiments into the mouth of Helena, who comically compares herself and Hermia to a spaniel (II.1.203), a bear (II.2.100) and a vixen (III.2.324).

MALE AUTHORITY

The play is certainly not feminist in its assumptions. This is hardly surprising, given the social position of women in the sixteenth century. Moreover, it is a play by a male author and in the original production the female parts would have been played by men. The drama begins with Theseus speaking of how he conquered the female society of the Amazons by force. Later Oberon conquers Titania by a hideous trick, while Lysander and Demetrius desert, insult and threaten the women who love them – events which the audience are expected to find humorous. Hermia and Helena achieve the husbands they desire only because the authority of Oberon and Theseus, greater male power figures, overrules that of Egeus. Once Hermia and Helena are married and in their role as wives, they cease to contribute any dialogue. Their marriages are finally blessed by the most authoritative male in the play, Oberon. In keeping with this emphasis on male authority, mention is made of the young women's fathers, Egeus and Nedar, but not their mothers. The only mother referred to in the whole play is the 'votress' who dies before the drama has begun.

WOMEN'S FRIENDSHIPS

Male and female are so opposed in the play that even the accounts of the 'changeling boy' are biased by gender, Robin stating that the child was stolen from an Indian king, Titania that his mother left him an orphan. Titania's attachment to the boy actually seems less motivated by affection for him than by love for his late mother. She speaks of how the two women shared the experience of the votress's pregnancy and mocked the merchant ships, **symbols** of male authority. Such all-female groupings are portrayed as happy ones, but not allowed to persist. Hippolyta has to leave her fellow Amazons, and although Helena reminds Hermia of their loving girlhood together, her nostalgic picture of their pre-adolescent happiness is soon dispelled by their quarrels over men.

CHECK THE BOOK A03

For a wide-ranging critical discussion of Shakespeare's representation of women, with particular reference to the fact that all the women's parts in his plays were originally played by men, see Dympna C. Callaghan, *Shakespeare Without Women* (Routledge, 2000).

STUDY FOCUS: SYMPATHY FOR WOMEN   A02

Substantial as the play's gender bias may be, we should not overstate it. The play celebrates marriage, not male dominance, even if the male is conceived of as the superior partner. Titania's rebellion against her husband is portrayed sympathetically, as is Hermia's rebellion against her father. When Theseus tells Hermia, 'To you your father should be as a god' (I.1.47), the audience are unlikely to share his opinion of that blustering personage, and the play contains many examples of laughable behaviour by male figures, including Oberon. Oberon's own reference to Queen Elizabeth (II.1.158) reminds us that this largely male-dominated society was ruled by a powerful and respected queen. While it may be true that the play depicts male superiority as more 'natural' than female superiority, it also offers us many female points of view and shows males and females interacting with each other in a variety of ways, with the females often highly sympathetic and assertive. We could argue that marriage in the play is depicted not as a closed institution with a simple set of rules which must be followed, but as a relationship which is always developing and has constantly to be negotiated afresh.

KEY QUOTATION: GENDER   A01

Helena complains that she has to chase after Demetrius: 'Apollo flies, and Daphne holds the chase, / The dove pursues the griffin, the mild hind / Makes speed to catch the tiger' (II.1.231–3).

Possible interpretations:

- Helena says that for a woman to chase a man is as unnatural as for a victim to chase a predator.

- She sees women as passive victims and herself as a humiliated exception.

- Nonetheless, all the women in the play take the initiative with men and Helena's extravagant behaviour makes her sympathetic as well as laughable.

CHECK THE BOOK   A03

Shakespeare's most conspicuous and apparently sexist treatment of the gender theme is his comedy *The Taming of the Shrew*, in which Petruchio wagers that he can win the obedience of the aggressive Katherina. Once he has tamed and married her, she proclaims, 'Such duty as the subject owes the prince, / Even such a woman oweth to her husband' (V.2.155–6). Critics still dispute whether her speech is to be taken at face value.

THEATRE

THEATRICAL ILLUSION

A Midsummer Night's Dream is a play which asks us to 'believe' that any number of things are happening before our eyes when plainly they are not: the stage is a palace in one scene and a wood in the next; it can even become several parts of the wood at once. Told that Oberon is invisible and Cobweb tiny enough to take on a bee in single combat, we behave rather like the lovers with the juice on their eyes and see what we are told to see – despite Shakespeare's repeatedly drawing our attention to the trick. When, for example, Quince points at the stage and says, 'This green plot shall be our stage' (III.1.3), we find ourselves thinking of the stage as a green plot, then as a stage, then as a green plot again, while all the time our eyes literally see a stage. When Francis Flute appears as Thisbe, we are reminded that the female characters were not played by women when Shakespeare's play was first staged, but by talented young men in 'drag'.

THE ROLE OF THE AUDIENCE

Each appearance by Peter Quince and his company is a reminder to us that any play requires not only skilful acting but a sympathetic audience. In the case of 'Pyramus and Thisbe' an audience full of 'self affairs' and actors who lack skill impede the performance. Even so, Hippolyta has to confess that she cannot resist Bottom's **tragic** turn: 'Beshrew my heart, but I pity the man' (V.1.274). In the contrasting case of *A Midsummer Night's Dream*, the audience constantly has a mixed state of awareness, a kind of waking dreaming, which allows them to see what is literally before their eyes and, at the same time, what the playwright wishes it to represent.

DO PLAYS JUST IMITATE REALITY?

One effect of repeatedly drawing our attention to the artificiality of the play is to show that it is more than a simple imitation of reality. We might think that only naïve performers like Quince and company could believe that the audience will mistake their acting for 'real life' and will panic at the entry of a bumpkin in a lion costume. But Theseus makes the same mistake when he says of actors, 'The best in this kind are but shadows' (V.1.205). Since a shadow conveys only a vague, passive image, a play made of shadows can be nothing more than a rough impression of the kinds of things which happen in real life. If such realism had been Shakespeare's goal in *A Midsummer Night's Dream*, surely his play would not have contained fairies, invisibility, magic juice, a man with the head of an ass and characters from ancient legends such as Theseus himself.

IMAGINATIVE TRANSFORMATION

In the epilogue (V.1.401) Robin revives the expression 'shadows'. The puck's phrase 'we shadows' seems at first to refer to himself and the fairies as nocturnal (echoing his earlier address to Oberon as 'King of Shadows', III.2.347), but soon comes to be understood as a reference to the acting company also. Is the actor playing Robin conceding that he and his colleagues are crude imitators of real life like Peter Quince? Or is he identifying the actors with some of the qualities of the fairies – dream-like creatures who first observe the mortal world from a distance, then intervene in it ('I'll be an auditor – An actor too, perhaps, if I see cause', III.1.62–3)? Or is his position somewhere between the two, hinting that a play is both an imitation of life and a creative transformation of it which draws upon those imaginative aspects of the mind which are experienced during dreams?

STUDY FOCUS: THE PLAY'S RELEVANCE `A02`

In interpreting the play, we may be in a similar position to the Athenian aristocrats when they watch 'Pyramus and Thisbe'. They complacently believe themselves to be spectators at a silly diversion which has no relevance to their own lives. We, however, know that the Athenian lovers have been in as potentially tragic a situation as Pyramus and Thisbe and that to some degree their own behaviour has been scripted by forces whose existence they deny: the fairies. Could any of this have an application to us? We are certainly not characters in a Shakespeare play, nor are we controlled by invisible fairies, but our lives, too, are shaped by forces beyond our control. Some people may, like the Elizabethans, locate such forces in the stars or divine predestination, others refer to genetic disposition, statistical probability or social conditioning, but the effect is the same. 'All the world's a stage, / And all the men and women merely players' (*As You Like It* II.7.140–1).

THE VISION OF *A MIDSUMMER NIGHT'S DREAM*

Because *A Midsummer Night's Dream* does not emphasise discussions about life and art, it is easy to mistake it for a lightweight entertainment. It does something much more skilful and satisfying, however, by integrating such ideas into the action, so that we see for ourselves the similarities between theatre and other human experience, and ourselves become part of the theatrical process. Through a kind of shared dream, mixing common experience and fantasy, Shakespeare creates worlds which parallel those normally experienced by the audience, celebrating, challenging, mocking and enriching the lives of anyone prepared to share what the epilogue calls 'these visions' (V.1.404).

KEY QUOTATION: THEATRE `A01`

Theseus is puzzled by the description of the craftsmen's play: 'Merry and tragical? Tedious and brief? / That is hot ice and wondrous strange snow! / How can we find the concord of this discord?' (V.1.58–60).

Possible interpretations:

- The description of the play is incoherent because Peter Quince has muddled the words.
- The play is meant to be a tragedy but it is so bad that the audience respond to it as a **comedy**.
- Shakespeare is hinting to us that he likes to mix comedy and tragedy which demands an alert and flexible response from his audience, not the smug and obvious reactions with which Theseus and his court react to 'Pyramus and Thisbe'.

CRITICAL VIEWPOINT `A04`

Shakespeare's bringing together of the merry and the tragical in a single play troubled early critics because it went against classical precedent. However, it was decisively defended on grounds of realism by Samuel Johnson in his *Preface to Shakespeare* (1765). Johnson proclaims that 'there is always an appeal open from criticism to nature' and praises the playwright's skilful 'interchange of seriousness and merriment … as he commands us, we laugh or mourn.'

STRUCTURE

THE THREE-PART PLOT

Seventeenth- and eighteenth-century productions took advantage of the three distinct elements of the play to prioritise the clowning of Bottom and the craftsmen, play down the fairies and cut out most of the lovers' story. Even in the nineteenth century the fairies' and lovers' scenes remained heavily cut. Significantly, it was only when the original interaction of the three plots was restored in the twentieth century that the play gained recognition as one of Shakespeare's masterpieces.

Underlying *A Midsummer Night's Dream* is the simple three-part structure characteristic of most **comedies**: 1) events go wrong, 2) there are ridiculous complications, 3) events go right. Shakespeare builds a more elaborate structure on this foundation, however, by telling three stories and developing them alongside each other: the misadventures of the four lovers, the conflict between Titania and Oberon, and the craftsmen's struggles to stage 'Pyramus and Thisbe'. The tension between Hippolyta and Theseus is a fourth, less prominent, plot element which helps to link the other three. The plots are also linked by interaction between the groups of characters, and by **themes** and parallel situations.

As the play progresses, the plots unfold at different speeds and our interest shifts between them. The lovers' conflicts are introduced in the first scene, reach a crescendo in Act III and are over by Act IV. The fairies' dispute first appears in Act II but, again, is resolved by Act IV. Finally, in Act V the craftsmen move to the centre of the action when their play, apparently wrecked in Act III, is staged successfully after all. These shifts between plots make *A Midsummer Night's Dream* much less straightforward to interpret than it may at first appear. Is it a play about love, as it seems at the start, or imagination, as becomes more apparent towards the end?

SETTING

Enid Welsford comments, 'The plot is a pattern … rather than a series of events occasioned by human character and passion, and this pattern, especially in the moonlit parts of the play, is a dance' (*The Court Masque*, 1927). Do you find the dance comparison an insightful one?

The structure of the play is supported, but also further complicated, by its settings: day and night, Athens and the wood. The conflict between the lovers starts in daytime Athens. The action then moves to the wood at night, where everyone's problems become more and more absurd. (Appropriately, 'wood' could mean 'crazy' in Elizabethan English).

Fortunately, the wood also proves to be a place of magical transformation where the fairies put everything right. The lovers return to the normality of daytime Athens to recover and be married, but then stay up till midnight to enjoy another encounter with the ridiculous, courtesy of the craftsmen's play, followed by the fairies' nocturnal blessing.

STUDY FOCUS: SUBSTITUTION

Titania complains that, due to her quarrel with Oberon, the seasons have changed places (II.1.111–4). Such swapping occurs throughout the play. Demetrius tries to substitute Hermia for Helena. Egeus tries to substitute Demetrius for Lysander. Bottom wants to become all the characters in 'Pyramus and Thisbe'. The puck eagerly takes on roles from animals and fire to the voices of Lysander and Demetrius. The puck substitutes Bottom for the Indian boy, but Titania then substitutes Bottom as her lover for Oberon. Swapping also helps to structure the play and give it unity. The Athenian court by day is succeeded by the fairy court at night, where Titania and Oberon give expression to the half-spoken tension between Hippolyta and Theseus. The craftsmen's play **parodies** the tragic fate that might have befallen the lovers earlier in the play.

FORM

THE ELIZABETHAN THEATRE

Shakespeare's plays were written for an Elizabethan stage, not a modern one. In a modern theatre, the worlds of the spectators and of the actors are sharply distinguished: in the dark auditorium the audience sits silent and receptive; on the lighted stage the actors move and perform. (The distinction is even more marked in the cinema.) In the Elizabethan theatre, this distinction did not exist so firmly, and for two reasons: first, performances took place in the open air and in daylight which illuminated everyone equally; secondly, the spectators were all around the stage (and wealthier spectators sometimes actually on it), and were dressed no differently to the actors, who wore contemporary dress. (An exception to this would be supernatural characters, such as the fairies in *A Midsummer Night's Dream*, who would have worn costumes inspired by folklore.) In such a theatre, spectators would be as aware of each other as of the actors; they could not lose their identity in a corporate group, nor could they ever forget that they were spectators at a performance. There was no chance that they could believe 'this is really happening'.

Most modern drama seeks to persuade us that what we are reading or watching is really happening. This is a kind of realism quite foreign to Shakespeare. If we try to read him like this, we shall find ourselves irritated by the improbabilities of his **plot**, confused by his chronology, puzzled by locations, frustrated by unanswered questions and dissatisfied by the motivation of the action. There is a great deal of psychological accuracy in Shakespeare's plays, but we are far from any attempt at realism.

This was communal theatre, not only in the sense that it was going on in the middle of a crowd but in the sense that the crowd might not arrive on time, keep quiet or remain for the whole performance. They might even interrupt or try to join in. Plays were preceded and followed by jigs and clowning, like the bergomask dance at the end of *A Midsummer Night's Dream*. It was all much more like our experience of a pantomime, and at a pantomime we are fully aware, and are meant to be aware, that we are watching games being played with reality.

> **CHECK THE BOOK** **A03**
>
> An authoritative book about the theatre of Shakespeare's time is Andrew Gurr's *The Shakespearean Stage* (Cambridge University Press, 1992).

THE AUDIENCE ACKNOWLEDGED

Elizabethan plays acknowledge the presence of the audience. It is addressed not only by prologues, epilogues and choruses, but in **soliloquies**. There is no realistic reason why characters like Helena at the end of Act I Scene 1 should suddenly explain their thoughts and feelings to empty rooms, but, of course, it is not an empty room. The actor is surrounded by people. Soliloquies are not addressed to the world of the play: they are for the audience's benefit. And that audience's complicity is assumed: when a character like Oberon declares himself to be invisible, it is accepted that he is.

CHECK THE BOOK   A03

Shakespeare's use of 'discrepant awareness' for comic effect in his plays, including *A Midsummer Night's Dream*, is thoroughly explored by Bertrand Evans in *Shakespeare's Comedies* (Clarendon Press, 1960).

Elizabethan plays are aware of themselves as dramas; in critical terminology, they are self-reflexive, commenting upon themselves as dramatic pieces and prompting the audience to think about the theatrical experience. They do this not only through their direct address to the audience but through their fondness for the play-within-a-play like 'Pyramus and Thisbe' (which reminds the audience that the encompassing play is also a play) and their constant use of **images** from, and **allusions** to, the theatre, such as the puck's 'I'll be an auditor, / An actor too perhaps, if I see cause' (III.1.62–3). They are fascinated by role playing, by acting, appearance and reality.

INFLUENCES ON SHAKESPEAREAN COMEDY

One of Shakespeare's key influences is classical Roman **comedy**, especially the plays of Plautus which he would have studied at school. These were often set in Athens. They told stories of lovers overcoming some kind of obstacle and were peopled by **stock characters** such as wayward sons, harsh fathers and artful slaves. Shakespeare downplays the scheming slaves, though the puck does retain something of this role, and retains the thwarted lovers. Having two pairs of lovers makes for more entertaining complications and Shakespeare uses this feature in several of his plays. Shakespeare sometimes departs from his Roman models by including scenes set in a pastoral world like the Forest of Arden in *As You Like It*, an alternative reality where the rules of everyday life do not seem to apply. Shakespeare's comedies are also likely to add an element of magic which was a popular device in earlier English dramas such as Peele's *Old Wives' Tale* and Lyly's *Endymion*. All these features can readily be seen in *A Midsummer Night's Dream*.

CONTEXT   A04

The Old Wives' Tale by George Peele was first printed in 1595, John Lyly's *Endymion* in 1591; both plays had been staged some time beforehand. Peele's drama is a play within a play, featuring multiple plots, a woodland setting and tales of magic. Lyly's play is about a man who falls in love with the moon goddess and is put into a magic sleep by his jealous former girlfriend, the story ending with several marriages. Shakespeare seems to have taken ideas from both of these sources.

STUDY FOCUS: COMIC CONVENTIONS   A02

In a comedy we expect foolish characters, ridiculous situations and, of course, a happy ending. The dramatist is likely to spread interest over several characters, not focus in depth on a limited number as he does in **tragedies** like *Hamlet* or *Macbeth*. Perhaps the most distinctive feature of Shakespeare's comedy is 'discrepant awareness', a form of **dramatic irony** where some characters have the benefit of knowing more than others, but the audience have the last laugh as they know more than everyone in the play. For example, the puck is invisible to the mortals in the forest and we enjoy watching the tricks he is able to play, but when he puts the magic juice on the eyes of the wrong man, we also enjoy his mistake. His confident boasting of his success is enjoyably ironic because we know that when Demetrius appears, as he does straight afterwards, the puck is going to become a victim of his own prank. His disconcerted admission, 'This is the woman, but not this the man' (III.2.42), confirms our expectation and, when our attention returns to him after the confrontation between Demetrius and Hermia, we find him trying to talk his way out of a serious telling off by Oberon. In some productions this is made more comical by Oberon tapping the puck with his sceptre, shaking him upside down or ducking his head in a pool of water.

REVISION FOCUS: TASK 6   A03

How far do you agree with the statements below?

- Written for the Elizabethan theatre, the play may seem out of place on today's stage.
- There are no great parts for actors in *A Midsummer Night's Dream*.

Try writing opening paragraphs for essays based on these discussion points. Set out your arguments clearly.

LANGUAGE

RHYME

As in all Shakespeare's plays, the characters mainly speak in **blank verse**, with rhyming **couplets** used to mark an exit or the end of a scene. Because many lines are **end-stopped**, placing emphasis on the final word, it is easy for both the Athenian nobles and the fairies to move from blank verse into couplets or some other rhyme scheme. This extra rhyming can have a variety of functions. At the end of the opening scene, for example, it serves to distance us from the lovers' experience; in Act II Scene 2 and Act III Scene 2 it makes the male lovers' declarations seem stilted and pompous; in Act III Scene 1 it points up the contrast between the exotic Titania and the prosaic Bottom.

STUDY FOCUS: SONG AND MUSIC — A02

The fairies make particular use of rhyme when uttering spells and charms or carrying out supernatural actions. All of their short-lined passages are rhymed, giving them a chanted, song-like quality. The fairies' lullaby for Titania in Act II Scene 2 is an actual song and it is possible that some of the other passages were also meant to be sung,

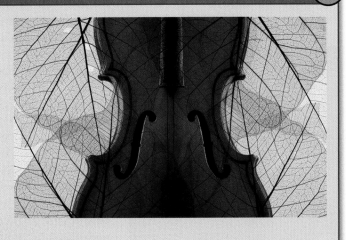

especially the various spells, and perhaps even the lines which are uttered by Robin, Oberon and Titania before their departure in Act IV Scene 1. The fairies' final blessing in Act V Scene 1 entails singing and dancing, but the text as we have it does not seem to contain the words they sing, unless we consider that lines 381–90 should themselves be set to music – which (with lines 411–12 added at the end) was the solution adopted by Mendelssohn (see below).

Its highly patterned **plot** and many theatrical effects make the play a particularly suitable one for music. Even in Shakespeare's lifetime music seems to have been added at the end of Act III (see **Part Five: Critical debates**). Purcell soon turned the play into an opera and Mendelssohn produced an outstanding accompaniment in his *Overture* and *Incidental Music* (1827/1843). Mendelssohn provides detailed orchestral accompaniment to the action of the play and sets two songs, 'Ye spotted snakes' (II.2.9) and 'Through the house' (V.1.369).

Duke Ellington's Shakespearean jazz album, *Such Sweet Thunder*, includes the composition 'Up and Down, Up and Down (I Will Lead Them Up and Down)' in which pairs of musicians take the roles of the couples in the wood and the trumpet imitates the intonation of the puck. Benjamin Britten's opera continued the tradition into the 1960s.

Decades earlier, Bernard Shaw had pointed out that the play is 'operatic' in its very nature with duets between characters, as they combine to create a mood and share ideas: for example, Theseus and Hippolyta's debate about the moon in the opening eleven lines, Lysander and Hermia's lament for the fate of lovers (I.1.132–55), or Robin and Oberon's conversation about spirits and the dawn (III.2.378–93). There are also 'arias' for individual characters, speeches where the action seems to stand still for passages of conspicuous beauty: among them, Titania's 'These are the forgeries of jealousy' (II.1.81–117), Oberon's 'I know a bank where the wild thyme blows' (II.1.249–56), and Helena's 'We, Hermia, like two artificial gods' (III.2.203–19).

THE CRAFTSMEN'S SPEECH

CHECK THE BOOK **A03**

For a fuller discussion of the 'stylistic multiplicity' of the play, see the chapter on 'Character and Language' in Peter Hollindale's *Penguin Critical Study* of *A Midsummer Night's Dream* (1992).

The craftsmen vary the tone and rhythm of the play by speaking in **prose** – although Bottom still manages his own kind of 'aria' at the end of Act IV Scene 1 – except in their dire efforts to perform in rhyming **verse**, which parody the techniques Shakespeare uses so brilliantly elsewhere. Short, rhymed lines and **alliteration** fail conspicuously in 'Pyramus and Thisbe' because the formal patterning and the meaning are so at odds with each other.

WORD PATTERNS AND MEANING

Lists are a common feature of the play, as Shakespeare works to create the details of new worlds in our imagination. Egeus lists the love tokens bestowed on his daughter. Oberon lists the beasts with which Titania might fall in love. Hermia and Lysander list the obstacles to love. The fairies offer Bottom a list of gifts.

'Therefore' is a particularly favoured conjunction, as the characters rationalise their way through the fantastic events by insisting on logical connections between them, sometimes

persuasively, sometimes not. When we hear that Theseus can see through 'saucy and audacious eloquence', 'therefore' he appreciates what is genuine (V.1.103–4), and that Oberon, seeing a fight is about to begin, 'therefore' sends Robin to prevent it (III.2.355), it is hard to fault their logic. Demetrius's argument to Helena, 'I love thee not, therefore pursue me not', is equally logical, but futile in the context of her passion (II.1.188). Titania's assertions that she has quarrelled with Oberon, '[t]herefore' the winds and the moon have reacted angrily, is beyond our understanding, although we accept it for the sake of the play (II.1.103). Snout's view that Snug dressed as a lion will terrify the audience, '[t]herefore' there should be a prologue on the subject, is less than convincing (III.1.27). Lysander's statement to Hermia that he agrees they should patiently bear their affliction, '[t]herefore' they should elope, makes no sense at all, but we happily go along with it, as does she (I.1.156).

Overall, we may say that the language of the play is always forming beautiful patterns, but that their relation to the 'real world' is never clear, for the focus of the play is not so much on objective reality as on the characters' changing perceptions of it.

IMAGERY AND SYMBOLISM

DARKNESS

Only one scene of the play (Act IV Scene 1) takes place in the clear light of day. As its title implies, the rest of *A Midsummer Night's Dream* is set at night or indoors. Before the invention of street-lighting, natural darkness was a much more common experience than it is today, and Shakespeare's original audience would have readily conceived of a moonlit wood as a place where people were out of their element, blundering and apprehensive – a highly suitable place to explore the mysteries of love and nature, since these may also, in their own way, leave us unsure of our ground.

MOONLIGHT

Elizabethan plays were acted in daylight, or indoors by the light of flaming torches – in either case, with little or no scenery – so speech had to be used to evoke scenic detail in the imaginations of the audience. In the case of *A Midsummer Night's Dream* repeated references to the moon conjure up in the mind's eye a mysterious, gentle light which transforms everything upon which it falls. However, the lunar references have more significance than the establishment of a magical atmosphere, important though that may be. The moon is also used to suggest a range of ideas which are of **thematic** relevance to the play.

STUDY FOCUS: THE MOON | A02

There was a long-standing belief still current in Elizabethan times that, while the heavens were as God had created them, perfect and unchanging, the fall of man had made the area from the moon down to the earth – the 'sublunary' world – imperfect and unstable. Hence change, decay and death could not be avoided in our world, and earthly love, in contrast to divine love, would often prove unreliable and impermanent. In Act II Scene 2 of *Romeo and Juliet*, Juliet cautions Romeo against swearing by the 'inconstant moon / That monthly changes in her circled orb'. As a **symbol** of inconstancy and imperfection, the moon is clearly relevant to the rapidly changing allegiances of Demetrius and Lysander. As the 'governess of floods' (II.1.103), the changing moon has a mysterious rhythmic affinity, not only with the tides, but with the female fertility cycle, and it can be associated with other cyclic and broadly predictable changes like the succeeding of the generations.

GRADE BOOSTER A03

If you are writing about the staging and acting of the play, remember that no one version is the definitive interpretation. Think about the various ways that the lines might be perfomed and show awareness that you are discussing one possibility among several. You may also need to refer specifically to the different ways that the play might have been staged in Shakespeare's day and today.

LUNAR TIME

In a sense the whole play runs to lunar time. Lysander has charmed Hermia by moonlight and sets the time of their elopement by the moon. Theseus and Hippolyta reckon the time left until their marriage by the moon's phases, Titania's fairy and Oberon measure their speed against the moon. Hermia measures her incredulity against the likelihood of the moon passing through the centre of the earth, Quince arranges his rehearsals for moonlight, and Pyramus cannot die until the moon has sympathetically withdrawn from the stage.

Although characters constantly refer to the moon, the nature of that moon is inconsistent, changing, like love, with the eye of the beholder. Theseus confidently announces in Act I Scene 1 that the new moon will not be seen until his wedding to Hippolyta in four days' time, but the moon seems to be shining brightly that very night and the wedding itself arrives in a mere two days. It is true that Shakespeare often disregards such minor details of continuity which are unlikely to be noticed in theatrical performance, but it is also true that the moonlit world of Acts II to IV is deeply disorientating and irrational. We could not expect anything else, since lunacy is by definition 'a state brought on by the moon'.

AMBIGUOUS SYMBOLS

All this seems complicated, and perhaps is, but fortunately the play does not spell out these matters or expect us to reflect upon them explicitly. The moon is simply a **symbol** with several associations – madness, chastity and fertility – all of which are relevant to the **themes** of the play. The moon's presence evokes these three states, but it is left to the characters to experience them and to the audience to decide how they may be linked.

STUDY FOCUS: THE MOON GODDESS A02

Several critics have suggested that Hippolyta's opening reference to 'the moon – like to a silver bow' (I.1.9), an **image** likely enough to occur to a bow-carrying Amazon, would also suggest to an educated Elizabethan the image of Diana, the goddess of hunting and of chastity. 'Dian's bud' (IV.1.70) is the apt name which Oberon gives the antidote to the magic juice. Diana was generally identified with the moon goddess Phoebe (I.1.209), as she is by Theseus when he warns Hermia that as a celibate nun at 'Diana's altar' (I.1.89) she would have to chant hymns to 'the cold fruitless moon' (I.1.73). Oberon later associates them again when he speaks of Elizabeth, the Virgin Queen, being defended by 'the chaste beams of the watery moon' (II.1.162).

Although chastity has to be spoken of with respect when it is associated with the queen of England, the play's preferred goal is marriage and it pointedly opens by celebrating a defeat of chastity: Theseus's martial and marital victories over Hippolyta, queen of the celibate Amazons. Hippolyta's image of a bow ready to fire calls to mind not only Diana, but Cupid, who is mentioned not long after by Helena (I.1.235). Paradoxically, Diana herself is the goddess of fertility as well as chastity.

EYES AND SIGHT

A Midsummer Night's Dream refers to the moon more frequently than any other Shakespeare play. The same applies to a second key image: that of eyes. Eyes are associated with sexual attraction, both for how they appear and for what they see. Helena's plea to Hermia, 'O, teach me how you look' (I.1.192) forcefully combines both meanings. Eyes are also associated with subjectivity. The wood at night is a place where eyes cannot operate as effectively as their owners would like – darkness 'from the eye his function takes' and 'doth impair the seeing sense' (III.2.177–9) – so that the encounters in the wood become representative of the encounters of love in general, where what we feel about someone is more important than the simple facts of what we see. As Helena puts it, 'Love looks not with the eyes, but with the mind, / And therefore is winged Cupid painted blind' (I.1.234–5). Reversing the process, it is to the eyes that the magic juice is applied, changing perception and, by so doing, changing feeling. Confronted by Lysander's altered allegiance, Hermia threatens to retaliate by scratching out Helena's offending eyes.

THE MAGIC JUICE

The effect of the magic juice is to speed up the process of falling in and out of love so that it comes to seem absurd. Nonetheless, while we are invited to laugh at the lovers, we are not expected to condemn them. It is part of the human condition that the inner world of our feelings and the outer world of external facts can be difficult to bring into harmony or even to speak about meaningfully. This uncertain relationship between what our senses detect and what our minds make of it is comically reflected in Quince's clumsy description of how Pyramus goes 'but to see a noise that he heard' (III.1.73–4) and Bottom's efforts when playing Pyramus to 'hear ... Thisbe's face' (V.1.188).

STUDY FOCUS: BOTTOM'S DREAM SPEECH   A03

Such sensory dislocation is carried to an extreme when Bottom attempts to formulate his experiences in the wood at night: 'The eye of man hath not heard, the ear of man hath not seen, man's hand is not able to taste, his tongue to conceive, nor his heart to report what my dream was!' (IV.1.205–7). What are we to make of this speech? Everyone who has studied the play agrees that the speech is based on St Paul's first letter to the Corinthians in the Bible (see **Part Two: Act IV Scene 1**), but the significance of the reference remains open to interpretation. Frank Kermode, writing in 1961, proposes that Bottom has experienced a religious revelation of a love beyond human expression. Peter Hollindale (1992) agrees that Bottom's words are a moving testimony to his experiences, but notes that they are still laughably confused and comical. Annabel Patterson (1989), in contrast, thinks Shakespeare is hinting at some later verses of St Paul's letter, which suggest that everyone in the community is of equal value, so smuggling a political message into the play. Louis Montrose (1995) takes a similar view, but this time citing earlier verses of St Paul's letter which indicate that the more people have wealth and worldly power, the less they have wisdom and virtue. What do you think?

> ### CRITICAL VIEWPOINT A03
>
> To Helen Hackett, in her study of *A Midsummer Night's Dream* (1997), the play is one in which 'mysterious forces, elusive of rational control, are shown irresistibly turning human events and feelings aside from their planned courses' and the moon, a traditional symbol of heavenly influence, is accordingly invoked throughout. Does this seem to you a just comment?

TWO KINDS OF LOVE?

Some critics (notably Paul Olson in his essay, 'The Meaning of Court Marriage', 1957 – see Antony W. Price, ed. *Shakespeare: A Midsummer Night's Dream, A Casebook*, 1983 in **Part Five: Critical debates**) have argued that the play presents us with two kinds of love: the superficial physical attractions of the eye, represented by the magic juice, and the settled, mature affection of the mind. However, it is difficult to reconcile this simple opposition with the example of Demetrius, whose settled affection comes about precisely from the application of the juice. Ultimately, *A Midsummer Night's Dream* does not attempt to solve such philosophical questions, only to acknowledge that the nature of our own feelings can be a mystery to us and that we are, to a degree, driven by forces beyond our comprehension and control.

MYTHOLOGY

Before the rise of science, one of the main ways of coming to terms with such forces was mythology: stories of gods and other supernatural beings whose deeds created the world which we inhabit today. *A Midsummer Night's Dream* supplies us with a **parody** of mythology in the shape of the fairies and also contains many references to figures from classical mythology, as suits its setting in ancient Athens. References to, for example, the Fates, the Furies and Venus reinforce the impression of humans impelled by forces beyond their grasp. However, since the setting of the play shares some of the features of classical Greece and Elizabethan England, these learned and exotic references are balanced by homegrown images of English beasts, flowers and birds: 'a fat and bean-fed horse' (II.1.45), 'oxlips and the nodding violet' (II.1.250) and 'russet-pated choughs' (III.2.21).

Like a science fiction story, *A Midsummer Night's Dream* is set somewhere which is both like and unlike our own reality. Its world is both ancient Athens and Elizabethan England, night and day, common experience and fantastic dream. We are invited to enjoy its colourful differences to our own world, but also to think about any revealing similarities.

CHECK THE BOOK   **A04**

There are several reference books which offer useful guidance through the complexities of Greek and Roman mythology. Edward Tripp's *Dictionary of Classical Mythology* (1970) is one which presents its information in a particularly clear and thorough way.

PART FIVE: CONTEXTS AND CRITICAL DEBATES

HISTORICAL BACKGROUND

SHAKESPEARE AND THE ENGLISH RENAISSANCE

NOTHING BEYOND QUESTION

Shakespeare arrived in London at the start of a 'golden age' for English literature, a development in that cultural movement which since the nineteenth century has been called the Renaissance. Meaning literally 'rebirth', the word refers to a revival of artistic and intellectual endeavour which began in Italy in the fourteenth century. The rediscovery of many classical texts of Greece and Rome fostered a confidence in human reason and potential. The discovery of America demonstrated that the world was a larger and stranger place than had been thought. Arguments that the sun, not the earth, was the centre of our planetary system challenged the centuries-old belief that humans were at the centre of the cosmos. The political philosophy of Machiavelli seemed to cut politics free from morality. And the religious movements we know collectively as the Reformation broke with the Church of Rome and set the individual conscience, not church authority, at the centre of the religious life. Nothing, it seemed, was beyond questioning, nothing impossible.

Shakespeare's drama, too, questions the beliefs, assumptions and politics upon which Elizabethan society was founded. The conclusions of his **plots** endorse the status quo, as audience expectation and censorship required, yet figures of authority like Oberon in *A Midsummer Night's Dream* are often undercut by comic or **parodic** figures like Bottom and the fairies, and dissenting voices are repeatedly heard in the plays defying the established order, as Hermia does when she refuses to marry Demetrius.

THE STATE OF THE NATION

Renaissance culture was intensely nationalistic. Like Edmund Spenser, whose epic poem *The Faerie Queene* celebrated Queen Elizabeth I, Shakespeare is preoccupied with national identity. His history plays examine how modern England came into being through the conflicts of the fifteenth century. He is fascinated by the exercise of power, bringing critical perspectives to bear in particular on the royal court. It may be paralleled by a different world, revealing uncomfortable similarities. Its hypocrisy may be bitterly denounced and its self-seeking ambition represented disturbingly in the figure of a villain. Shakespeare is fond of displacing the court to another context, the better to examine its assumptions and pretensions and to offer alternatives to the courtly life (for example, in the nocturnal wood of *A Midsummer Night's Dream*).

The nationalism of the English Renaissance was reinforced by Henry VIII's break with Rome. Because the Pope excommunicated Queen Elizabeth and relieved English Catholics of their allegiance to the Crown, there was deep suspicion of them as potential traitors, reinforced by the Spanish Armada of 1588 and, later, the Gunpowder Plot of 1605. Shakespeare's plays are remarkably free from direct religious sentiment, leading many to question where his religious sympathies, if any, lie. Some of his emphases are Protestant. Young women are destined for marriages, not nunneries, the fate with which Hermia is threatened in the opening scene of *A Midsummer Night's Dream*. On the other hand, this play contains fairies, a belief some Protestant thinkers condemned as a Papist superstition which needed to be stamped out. Setting the play before Christianity enables Shakespeare to sidestep such religious controversy.

> **CHECK THE BOOK** **A04**
>
> Michael Wood's *In Search of Shakespeare* (2003), a book based on his television series, examines the historical background in detail, including the evidence for Shakespeare's religious affiliations.

SHAKESPEARE'S THEATRE

THE DRAMATISTS

The theatre for which the plays were written was one of the most remarkable innovations of the Renaissance. There had been no theatres or acting companies during the medieval period. Plays had been almost exclusively religious, performed on carts and in open spaces at Christian festivals. Professional performers offered only mimes, juggling and comedy acts, in the yards of inns, on makeshift stages in market squares, or anywhere else suitable. They were regarded by officialdom and polite society as little better than vagabonds and layabouts.

Just before Shakespeare went to London all this began to change. A number of young men who had been to the universities of Oxford and Cambridge came to London in the 1580s and began to write plays which made use of what they had learned about the drama of ancient Greece and Rome. Plays such as John Lyly's *Alexander and Campaspe* (1584), Christopher Marlowe's *Tamburlaine the Great* (about 1587) and Thomas Kyd's *The Spanish Tragedy* (1588–9) were unlike anything that had been written in English before. They were full-length plays on secular subjects, taking their **plots** from history and legend, adopting many of the devices of classical theatre, and offering a range of **characterisation** and situation hitherto unattempted in English drama. With the exception of Lyly's **prose** pieces, they were in the unrhymed **iambic pentameters** (**blank verse**) which the Earl of Surrey had introduced into English earlier in the sixteenth century. This was a freer and more expressive medium than the rhymed **verse** of medieval drama.

PROFESSIONAL THEATRE

The most significant change of all, however, was that these dramatists wrote for the professional theatre. In 1576 James Burbage built the first permanent theatre in England, in Shoreditch, just beyond London's northern boundary. It was called simply 'The Theatre'. Others soon followed. Thus, when Shakespeare came to London, he met with a flourishing drama, theatres and companies of actors (all female parts in the Elizabethan theatre were taken by boys or men). His company performed at James Burbage's Theatre until 1596, then used the Swan and Curtain until they moved into their own new theatre, the Globe, in 1599. It was burned down in 1613 when a cannon was fired during a performance of Shakespeare's *Henry VIII*.

THE GLOBE

With the completion in 1996 of Sam Wanamaker's project to construct in London a replica of the Globe, a version of Shakespeare's theatre can now be experienced at first-hand. It is very different to the usual modern experience of drama. The form of the Elizabethan theatre derived from the inn yards and animal baiting rings in which actors had performed previously. They were circular wooden buildings with a paved courtyard in the middle, open to the sky. A rectangular stage jutted out into the middle of this yard. Some of the audience stood in the yard (or 'pit') to watch the play. They were thus on three sides of the stage, close up to it and on a level with it. These 'groundlings' paid only a penny to get in, but for wealthier spectators there were seats in three covered tiers or galleries, extending round most of the auditorium and overlooking the pit and the stage.

CHECK THE BOOK **A04**

For a detailed and dramatic account of the creation of the Globe, which included dismantling the old theatre against the opposition of the landowner, see James Shapiro's *1599: A Year in the Life of William Shakespeare* (2005).

STAGING PRACTICES

Such a theatre could hold about three thousand spectators. The yards were about 80ft in diameter and the rectangular stage approximately 40ft by 30ft and 5ft 6in high. Shakespeare aptly called such a theatre a 'wooden O' in the Prologue to *Henry V* (line 13). The stage itself was partially covered by a roof or canopy which projected from the wall at the rear of the stage and was supported by two posts at the front. This protected the stage and performers from inclement weather, and to it were secured winches and other machinery for stage effects. On either side at the back of the stage was a door. These led into the dressing room (or 'tiring house', mentioned by Peter Quince in *A Midsummer Night's Dream*, III.1.4) and it was by means of these doors that actors entered and left the stage. In Act II Scene 1 Oberon and Titania use them to enter from opposite sides and confront one another centre stage. Between the doors was a small recess or alcove which was curtained off. Such a 'discovery place' served, for example, for Titania's bower when in Act II Scene 2 and Act III Scene 1 of *A Midsummer Night's Dream* she lies sleeping on her flowery bed. Above the discovery place was a balcony, used for the famous balcony scenes of *Romeo and Juliet*. Actors also had access to the area under the stage; from here, in the 'cellarage', would have come the voice of the ghost of Hamlet's father (*Hamlet*, II.1.150–82).

SYMBOLIC SETTINGS

There was very little in the way of scenery or props – there was nowhere to store them (there were no wings in this theatre) nor any way to set them up (no tabs across the stage), and, in any case, productions had to be transportable for performance at court or at noble houses. The stage was bare, which is why characters often tell us where they are, as Quince does at the start of Act III Scene 1: there was nothing on the stage to indicate location. It is also why location is so often **symbolic**. It suggests a dramatic mood or situation, rather than a place: a wood at night can reflect the characters' relationships, a world of confusion from which they can find no escape, harbouring nasty surprises and also miraculous joys.

CONTINUOUS ACTION

None of the plays printed in Shakespeare's lifetime marks act or scene divisions. These have been introduced by later editors. The staging of Elizabethan plays was continuous, with the 'scenes' following one after another in quick succession. We have to think of a more fluid and much faster production than we are generally used to: in the prologues to *Romeo and Juliet* (line 12) and *Henry VIII* (line 13) Shakespeare speaks of only two hours as the playing time. It is because plays were staged continuously that exits and entrances are written in as part of the script: characters speak as they enter or leave the stage because otherwise there would be a silence while, in full view, they took up their positions. (This is also why dead bodies are carried off: they cannot get up and walk off.)

LITERARY BACKGROUND

ORIGINAL PUBLICATION

Nineteen of Shakespeare's plays were printed during his lifetime in books called 'quartos', each containing one play. Shakespeare, however, did not supervise their publication. This was not unusual. When a playwright had sold a play to a dramatic company he sold his rights in it: copyright belonged to whoever had possession of an actual copy of the text, and so consequently authors had no control over what happened to their work. Anyone who could get hold of the text of a play might publish it if they wished. Hence, what found its way into print might be the author's copy, but it might be an actor's copy or prompt copy, perhaps cut or altered for performance; sometimes, actors (or even members of the audience) might publish what they could remember of the text. Printers, working without the benefit of the author's oversight, introduced their own errors, through misreading the manuscript for example, and by 'correcting' what seemed to them not to make sense.

In 1623 John Heminges and Henry Condell, two actors in Shakespeare's company, collected together texts of thirty-six of Shakespeare's plays (*Pericles* was not included) and published them in a large book known as the First Folio, followed by later editions in 1632, 1663 and 1685. Despite the book's appearance of authority, the texts in the First Folio present many difficulties, for there are printing errors and confused passages in the plays, and its texts often differ significantly from those of earlier quartos, when these exist.

MODERN EDITIONS

Shakespeare's texts have, then, been through a number of intermediaries. We do not have his authority for any one of his plays, and hence we cannot know exactly what it was that he wrote. Bibliographers, textual critics and editors have spent a great deal of effort on endeavouring to get behind the errors, uncertainties and contradictions in the available texts to recover the plays as Shakespeare originally wrote them. What we read is the result of these efforts. Modern texts are what editors have constructed from the available evidence: they correspond to no sixteenth- or seventeenth-century editions, and to no early performance of a Shakespeare play. Furthermore, these composite texts differ from each other, for different editors read the early texts differently and come to different conclusions.

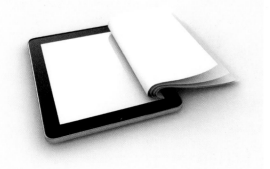

Often the judgements embody, if not the personal prejudices of the editor, then the cultural preferences of the time in which he or she was working. Growing awareness of this has led recent scholars to repudiate the attempt to construct a 'perfect' text. Stanley Wells and Gary Taylor, the editors of the Oxford edition of *The Complete Works* (1986), point out that almost certainly the texts of Shakespeare's plays were altered in performance, and from one performance to another, so that there may never have been a single version. They note, too, that Shakespeare probably revised and rewrote some plays. They do not claim to print a definitive text of any play, but prefer what seems to them the 'more theatrical' version, and when there is a great difference between available versions, as with *King Lear*, they print two texts.

ORIGINAL IDEAS

Shakespeare's usual practice in creating a play was to explore the dramatic potential of an existing story. However, the three interlinking tales of *A Midsummer Night's Dream* (the lovers in the forest, the quarrel between Titania and Oberon, the staging of a play by inexperienced craftsmen) all seem to be his own invention. The only other dramas in the Shakespeare canon which are thought to be similarly original are *Love's Labour's Lost* and *The Tempest*. *The Tempest*, although written about fifteen years after *A Midsummer Night's Dream*, exhibits several similarities. Like Oberon, Prospero is a domineering but well-meaning authority figure who directs the events to a positive outcome, while the contrast between the earthy Bottom and the playful spirit Robin is developed to a greater extreme in Caliban and Ariel. Both plays conclude with the suggestion that life is like a theatrical performance or a dream.

OVID'S METAMORPHOSES

If Shakespeare invented *A Midsummer Night's Dream*, he still took many of its ingredients from his reading. One major influence is Ovid's *Metamorphoses*, a book of **verse** which he knew in the original Latin and in English translation, having almost certainly studied it first at school. Ovid recounts myths and legends, in each of which a supernatural transformation occurs which accounts for some phenomenon in the natural world. The story of Pyramus and Thisbe is one such legend. The claim that it was the blood of the dying Pyramus splashing the mulberry tree which caused it to have a dark colour ever afterwards probably suggested Oberon's story that a hit from Cupid's arrow caused the dark colour of the pansy (II.1.155–68). Several other details in *A Midsummer Night's Dream* come from the *Metamorphoses*, including Titania's name and much of her speech about the disorder of the seasons in Act II Scene 1. Arthur Golding's rather awkward translation of the *Metamorphoses*, made in 1567, including such lines as, 'This said, she took the sword yet warm with slaughter of her love / And setting it beneath her breast, did to her heart it shove' probably suggested the inept **verse** of 'Pyramus and Thisbe'.

CHAUCER AND PLUTARCH

Shakespeare found the Theseus and Hippolyta **plot** in Chaucer's *The Knight's Tale*. *The Knight's Tale*, a story of two knights in love with the same lady at the court of Theseus, was retold in a play of 1613 called *The Two Noble Kinsmen*, which is thought to be a collaboration between Shakespeare and John Fletcher. In Chaucer's version, Theseus is styled the 'Duke' of Athens. The poem tells us that he has conquered, captured and wedded the Queen of the Amazons, called 'Ipolita' rather than the usual Antiope, and that he celebrates the occasion with a great feast. The rites of May, the duke's love of hunting with hounds and the names Philostrate and Egeus are all mentioned by Chaucer. Plutarch's *Life of Theseus*, as translated by Sir Thomas North in 1579, seems to have supplied additional details of Theseus's life.

CONTEXT A04

The Canterbury Tales by Geoffrey Chaucer was written in the later years of the fourteenth century and circulated in many manuscripts before being printed in 1478. It contains a wide range of stories, mostly in verse, supposedly told by pilgrims on the way to Canterbury.

THE SUPERNATURAL ELEMENTS

Much of the conception of the fairies must have come from folklore passed on by word of mouth, but some details, particularly those regarding Oberon, derive from a French romance called *Huon of Bordeaux*, which had been translated by Lord Berners between 1533 and 1542, then staged in a dramatised version in 1593, and from a book called *The Discovery of Witchcraft* by Reginald Scot (1584). Apuleius's *Transformations of Lucius* or *The Golden Ass* (a Latin tale of the second century, translated in 1566 by William Adlington) furnished the ideas of a man turned into an ass who is loved by a superior woman, the punishment of being made to fall in love with an unworthy object, and the recovery of one's true form after a transcendent vision.

PAGEANTS

CHECK THE BOOK **A04**

There are helpful evaluations of Shakespeare's sources in the New Cambridge edition edited by R.A. Foakes (1984) and in Peter Hollindale's Penguin Critical Study of the play (1992). There is a wide-ranging account of Shakespeare's literary sources in Harold Brooks's introduction to the Arden edition of *A Midsummer Night's Dream* (1979), which also reprints key extracts in an appendix.

Not all of Shakespeare's sources would have existed in the form of books, however. The folklore of the fairies has already been mentioned. The play was undoubtedly influenced also by the courtly pageants staged at country houses. Oberon seems to refer to one of these in the passage where he speaks of seeing 'a mermaid on a dolphin's back' (II.1.150; see **Part Two: Act II Scene 1**). At Elvetham in 1595, for example, the entertainments laid on for Queen Elizabeth included a water pageant and a group of dancing fairies who gave her a garland of flowers on behalf of 'Auberon the Fairy King'. When Shakespeare's fairies sing and dance, they are probably emulating such well-known occasions and bringing a scaled-down version of the spectacle to the theatre audience.

MAYING

A more widespread form of festivity, which also helped shape the play, is the 'rite of May' mentioned by Theseus at IV.1.130, when country folk went out into the woods and hills to celebrate the change of the seasons, particularly young people keen to elude the watchful eye of their elders (see **Part Three: Themes** on **Marriage**). Although 'Maying' was the general name for these customs, they could also be practised at Whitsun and other times of the year, so it is not out of place that Theseus should speak of the rite of May at the end of a midsummer night. Indeed, according to fairy folklore, the summer solstice was a particularly likely time for spirits to appear. Thus the central idea of the liberating night in the wood, when the marital destinies of the lovers are settled, and the fairies' presence is felt, is taken by Shakespeare, not from literary sources, but from popular tradition.

CRITICAL DEBATES

EARLY VIEWS AND ADAPTATIONS

A Midsummer Night's Dream was evidently popular in its author's lifetime. The title page of the first edition (1600) states that it had been 'sundry times publickely acted', a fact confirmed by Edward Sharpham's **comedy** *The Fleire*, performed in 1606, which refers familiarly to Thisbe's comical death scene. The text of *A Midsummer Night's Dream* was reprinted in 1619, then in the 1623 First Folio, where a new stage direction at the end of Act III, *'They sleep all the act'*, has been interpreted by some scholars as indicating a recent revival, since the 'act' seems to have been a musical interlude between scenes which was then newly fashionable.

During the republican period (1642–60), when the king had been executed and the country was under Puritan control, all plays were banned by the government. When the theatres reopened, Shakespeare's works naturally seemed old-fashioned in their language and staging (Samuel Pepys, having seen a 1662 production of the play, wrote in his diary that it 'was the most insipid ridiculous play that ever I saw in my life'. To appeal to audiences after the Restoration, the play was performed in adaptations, nine of which appeared between 1661 and 1816. In every one, the story was simplified and Shakespeare's careful balance between comedy, love and the supernatural overturned. The creation of character, scene and atmosphere through subtle language was overwhelmed by stunning visual and musical effects.

Purcell's opera *The Fairy Queen* (1692), for example, removed half the original text, cutting out Hippolyta and shifting 'Pyramus and Thisbe' to Act III to make way for a big finish, including an appearance by the goddess Juno drawn by peacocks. The actor David Garrick's 1755 adaptation, *The Fairies*, cut three quarters of the text, added twenty-seven songs and jettisoned the craftsmen. Traditionally, academics have condemned all this as cultural vandalism, but anyone who has enjoyed such imaginative adaptations of Shakespeare as the 1996 Baz Luhrmann film version of *Romeo and Juliet*, and for that matter the 1999 Michael Hoffman film version of *A Midsummer Night's Dream*, will recognise them as ways to make the play fit the production expectations of their day, and to be accessible and entertaining for a contemporary audience who, in past centuries, would not, after all, have studied Shakespeare in school.

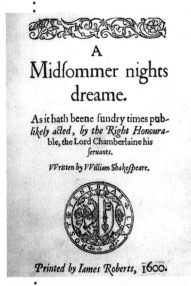

NINETEENTH- AND EARLY TWENTIETH-CENTURY THEATRE

An 1840 production can claim the credit for reinstating about eighty per cent of the original text. Thereafter, actors usually spoke Shakespeare's words, even if some of them were cut, but spectacular costumes, special effects and large amounts of music still predominated – in the second half of the nineteenth century the music normally being Mendelssohn's.

Harley Granville Barker's 1914 version was the first successfully to break with the post-Restoration norm, trying to shift the emphasis from the traditional spectacle to the words themselves. Barker replaced Mendelssohn with English folk music, elaborate sets with painted backdrops and delicate fairy costumes with strange gold-painted ones which (in the words of Desmond MacCarthy) made their wearers look 'as if they had been detached from some fantastic, bristling old clock'.

CHECK THE BOOK **A04**

Trevor R. Griffith's edition of the play in the 'Shakespeare in Production' series (Cambridge University Press, 1996) combines the text with a detailed account of how it has been staged and acted in a range of historic performances.

MODERN PRODUCTIONS

There have since been many attempts to present the play afresh while keeping to the original text, among the more radical an American production of 1958 which relocated the play in Texas with the Athenians as cowboys and Hippolyta as a Native American. The best-known of such productions, because of its systematic attempt to depart from previous stage practices, was Peter Brooks's 1970 version, which made the stage a white box furnished with trapezes and coiled wires, and introduced distinctly adult fairies. Hailed by some as an imaginative celebration of theatricality, dismissed by others as gimmickry, Brooks's staging certainly made the audience see the play in a new light, but in its way maintained the tradition of striking spectacle. Theatregoers wishing to see the fullest emphasis placed on the power of Shakespeare's text may find they are better served by small-scale amateur or semi-professional productions than by those designed to leave their mark on theatrical history.

LITERARY DEBATE

CHECK THE BOOK   A03

The volume on *A Midsummer Night's Dream* in the 'Casebook' series, edited by Antony W. Price (1983), anthologises many of the critics cited here, plus a large number of others. Another useful collection is the volume edited by Harold Bloom in the 'Modern Critical Interpretations' series (1987).

Critics in the eighteenth and nineteenth centuries saw the play only in productions which they considered to be heavy-handedly vulgar. They viewed it as a delicate piece of escapism, enjoyable but apparently unstageable, and not to be taken very seriously. Little detailed discussion was attempted until the twentieth century, when scholars set about trying to recover something of the original context and to reconstruct its character before it became an excuse for music and dance spectacle.

Studies of folklore such as Minor White Latham's *The Elizabethan Fairies* (1930) and Katherine Briggs's *The Anatomy of Puck* (1959) clarified the superstitions on which Shakespeare drew. C. L. Barber in *Shakespeare's Festive Comedy* (1959) related the play to May games, aristocratic pageants and the vogue for Ovid. Paul A. Olson in 'The Meaning of Court Marriage' (1957), William Rossky in 'Imagination in the English Renaissance' (1958) and R. W. Dent in 'Imagination in *A Midsummer Night's Dream*' (1964) interpreted the play in the light of Elizabethan views about the function of imagination. All three essays are included in Antony W. Price, ed., *Shakespeare: A Midsummer Night's Dream, A Casebook* (1983).

G. Wilson Knight's *The Shakespearean Tempest* (1932), H. B. Charlton's *Shakespearean Comedy* (1939) and John Russell Brown's *Shakespeare and his Comedies* (1957) integrated the play into the Shakespeare canon by tracing patterns of **imagery**, **plot** device and **theme** which link it to his other plays. Volumes wholly devoted to the play – David P. Young's *Something of Great Constancy* (1966) and Stephen Fender's *Shakespeare: A Midsummer Night's Dream* (1968) – stressed its complexities, showing that it is not simply a pantomime-style entertainment or a repository of Elizabethan beliefs, but a rich text in which the imagination unifies seeming opposites and in which transformation and **parody** challenge stock responses.

Jan Kott's *Shakespeare Our Contemporary* (1964) offered the most extreme reaction to the traditional view of the play as charming and insubstantial, claiming instead that it depicts a crazed and cruel world, driven by lust. Although refuted by many, Kott's views have certainly been influential (for example, on Peter Brooks's 1970 production) and initiated the late-twentieth-century vogue for 're-readings' of the play in the light of modern preoccupations.

CONTEMPORARY APPROACHES

FEMINIST READINGS

Critical approaches in recent decades have tended to focus on attitudes within the play, such as those towards gender and power, most liable to make a modern reader uneasy. Shirley Nelson Garner in 'Jack shall have Jill; / Nought shall go ill' (1981) interprets the play as a male–female power struggle, Louis Adrian Montrose's 'Shaping Fantasies' (1983, included, like Garner, in Richard Dutton, ed. *New Casebooks: A Midsummer Night's Dream*) relates the presentation of women to Elizabethan men's anxieties about female power, while Regina Buccola's *Fairies, Fractious Women and the Old Faith* (2006) stresses the play's sympathy for rebellious women.

NEW HISTORICIST AND MARXIST READINGS

New Historicists compare works of literature to non-literary writings of the same period in an attempt to understand their original contexts. This approach often overlaps with Marxist studies, which examine how literature has been shaped by class structure and social change. Elliot Krieger's *A Marxist Study of Shakespeare's Comedies* (1979) and Richard Wilson's 'The Kindly Ones: The Death of the Author in Shakespearean Athens' (1993, later revised in his book *Shakespeare in French Theory*, 2007) see the play as one which supports the outlook of the ruling class, while in *Shakespeare's Comedies* (2009) Kiernan Ryan argues that the effect of the play is to subvert aristocratic authority.

CARNIVALESQUE READINGS

Ryan combines a Marxist and a Dialogic approach (one which considers how a text can come to voice a range of competing points of view). It is sometimes argued that this 'polyphony' originated from festivities such as carnival. In *Shakespeare and the Popular Voice* (1989), Annabel Patterson suggests that Maying, marriage and the staging of a play are all festive occasions which help to legitimise the point of view of the craftsmen.

PSYCHOANALYTIC AND POST-STRUCTURALIST CRITICISM

Psychoanalytic or Freudian Criticism traces the psychological mechanisms by which meaning is created and distorted. Norman Holland in his 'Hermia's Dream' (1979) examines one speech in this light. James L. Calderwood in the 'New Critical Introductions to Shakespeare' series (1992) brings psychoanalytical and philosophical approaches to bear on a wide range of features, while Terence Hawkes in his book *Meaning by Shakespeare* (1993) challenges a number of received views. In their concern to open up the text to new readings, both of these critics could be labelled as practitioners of Post-Structuralism, which starts from the tenet that meaning is not simply inherent in words, but depends on their relation to larger systems of language and thought.

THEATRE STUDIES

Roger Warren's *A Midsummer Night's Dream* in the 'Text and Performances' series (1983) and Jay L. Halio's equivalent volume in the 'Shakespeare in Performance' series (1995) give stimulating accounts of performances on stage, television and film. Philip C. McGuire in the opening chapter of his book *Speechless Dialect: Shakespeare's Open Silences* (1985) examines how different stage productions have dealt with Hippolyta's silences, and so brings us full circle to Feminist concerns.

CRITICAL VIEWPOINT A03

Myth Criticism holds that all literature is ultimately based on myths explaining patterns in nature. In a chapter of *Northrop Frye on Shakespeare* (1986), Frye applies this to the structure of the **comic** plot, which he also relates to the custom of Maying and classical mythology.

CHECK THE BOOK A04

The 'New Casebook' volume edited by Richard Dutton (1996) includes pieces by many of the critics mentioned above. Helen Hackett's study in the 'Writers and their Work' series (1997) attempts to combine several contemporary approaches in a brief, accessible study.

PART SIX: GRADE BOOSTER

ASSESSMENT FOCUS

WHAT ARE YOU BEING ASKED TO FOCUS ON?

The questions or tasks you are set will be based around the four **Assessment Objectives**, **AO1** to **AO4**.

You may get more marks for certain **AOs** than others depending on which unit you're working on. Check with your teacher if you are unsure.

WHAT DO THESE AOS ACTUALLY MEAN?

	ASSESSMENT OBJECTIVES	MEANING?
AO1	Articulate creative, informed and relevant responses to literary texts, using appropriate terminology and concepts, and coherent, accurate written expression.	You write about texts in accurate, clear and precise ways so that what you have to say is clear to the marker. You use literary terms (e.g. **stock character**) or refer to concepts (e.g. **irony**) in relevant places.
AO2	Demonstrate detailed critical understanding in analysing the ways in which structure, form and language shape meanings in literary texts.	You show that you understand the specific techniques and methods used by the writer(s) to create the text (e.g. **imagery**, **antithesis**, etc.). You can explain clearly how these methods affect the meaning.
AO3	Explore connections and comparisons between different literary texts, informed by interpretations of other readers.	You are able to see relevant links between different texts. You are able to comment on how others (such as critics) view the text.
AO4	Demonstrate understanding of the significance and influence of the contexts in which literary texts are written and received.	You can explain how social, historical, political or personal backgrounds to the texts affected the writer and how the texts were read when they were first published and at different times since.

WHAT DOES THIS MEAN FOR YOUR STUDY OR REVISION?

Depending on the course you are following, you could be asked to:

- Respond to a general question about the text as a whole. For example:

Explore the ways that Shakespeare uses the magical features of *A Midsummer Night's Dream.*

- Write about an aspect of *A Midsummer Night's Dream* which is also a feature of other texts you are studying. These questions may take the form of a challenging statement or quotation which you are invited to discuss. For example:

How far do you agree that *A Midsummer Night's Dream* **is pure comic fantasy, untouched by any element of the tragic?**

- Or you may have to focus on the particular similarities, links, contrasts and differences between this text and others. For example:

Compare the dramatic techniques writers employ to produce comedy in *A Midsummer Night's Dream* **and other text(s) you have studied.**

EXAMINER'S TIP

Make sure you know how many marks are available for each **AO** in the task you are set. This can help to divide up your time or decide how much attention to give each aspect.

TARGETING A HIGH GRADE

It is very important to understand the progression from a lower grade to a high grade. In all cases, it is not enough simply to mention some key points and references – instead, you should explore them in depth, drawing out what is interesting and relevant to the question or issue.

TYPICAL C GRADE FEATURES

	FEATURES	EXAMPLES
A01	You use critical vocabulary accurately, and your arguments make sense, are relevant and focus on the task. You show detailed knowledge of the text.	*The simile 'I am as ugly as a bear' reminds us of Helena's lack of confidence in her own attractiveness and makes us feel sorry for her, yet her extravagant language also makes her comical. Her actions throughout this scene confirm the two responses.*
A02	You can say how some specific aspects of form, structure and language shape meanings.	*Puck's passing reference to the sleeping Titania in her 'cradle' creates suspense. We wonder if coming events will awake her and, if so, what will happen.*
A03	You consider, in detail, the connections between texts, and also how interpretations of texts differ, with some relevant supporting references.	*'Pyramus and Thisbe' is a hilarious performance, but the resemblance of the story to "Romeo and Juliet" is a reminder that the lovers of "A Midsummer Night's Dream" might have come to an equally tragic end.* *Like Prospero in Act I Scene 2 of "The Tempest", Oberon in Act II Scene 1 takes control of events in a way which can be seen as selfish or selfless.*
A04	You can write about a range of contextual factors and make some specific and detailed links between these and the task or text.	*In legend Theseus is a ruthless killer and faithless lover, so it is quite comical to find him represented here as a sober, responsible duke who has no belief in 'antique fables'.*

TYPICAL FEATURES OF AN A OR A* RESPONSE

	FEATURES	EXAMPLES
A01	You use appropriate critical vocabulary, technical terms and a clear, fluent style. Your arguments are well structured, coherent and always relevant, with a sharp focus on task.	*The other sub-plots having been resolved by the end of Act IV, the play's dramatic focus shifts to the craftsmen, with an accompanying shift of emphasis from the theme of love to a complementary one, which we may broadly describe as that of imagination.*
A02	You explore and analyse key aspects of form, structure and language, and evaluate perceptively how they shape meanings.	*When Theseus tells Hermia that she should regard her father 'as a god', he is emphasising her comparative lack of status and power, yet in so doing he signals her courage and unintentionally discredits Egeus, who cannot begin to live up to the comparison.*
A03	You show a detailed and perceptive understanding of issues raised through connections between texts and can consider different interpretations with a sharp evaluation of their strengths and weaknesses. You have a range of excellent supporting references.	*Shakespeare draws on Ovid's "Metamorphoses", a book which retells myths and legends of supernatural transformation. In contrast to Ovid, Shakespeare gives greatest emphasis to changes which represent growth – from child to adult, single person to spouse, rehearsal to performance. This pattern, as Hippolyta hints, unifies the events of the play into 'something of great constancy'.*
A04	You show deep, detailed and relevant understanding of how contextual factors link to the text or task.	*Oberon is a figure of male authority whose actions consistently demonstrate his desire to control women, yet he not only gives decisive support to Helena, he also refers respectfully to 'the imperial votress', a reminder that the mortal world outside the play was ruled by Queen Elizabeth I, whose authority no male could defy.*

HOW TO WRITE HIGH-QUALITY RESPONSES

The quality of your writing – how you express your ideas – is vital for getting a higher grade, and **AO1** and **AO2** are specifically about **how** you respond.

FIVE KEY AREAS

The quality of your responses can be broken down into **five** key areas.

1. THE STRUCTURE OF YOUR ANSWER /ESSAY

- First, get **straight to the point in your opening paragraph.** Use a sharp, direct first sentence that deals with a key aspect and then follows up with evidence or a detailed reference.
- **Put forward an argument or point of view** (you won't always be able to challenge or take issue with the essay question, but generally, where you can, you are more likely to write in an interesting way).
- **Signpost your ideas** with connectives and references, which help the essay flow.
- **Don't repeat points already made**, not even in the conclusion, unless you have something new to say that adds a further dimension.

EXAMINER'S TIP ✓

Answer the question set, not the question you'd like to have been asked. Examiners say that often students will be set a question on one character (for example, Oberon) but end up writing almost as much about another (such as the puck). Or, they write about one aspect from the question (for example, 'comic action') but ignore another (such 'serious themes'). **Stick to the question**, and answer **all parts of it**.

TARGETING A HIGH GRADE **A01**

Here's an example of an opening paragraph that gets straight to the point, addressing the question: **'Bottom may be foolish, but he is also the hero of the play.' How do you respond to this viewpoint?**

Bottom's foolishness cannot be denied. The puck quickly recognises him to be 'the shallowest thick-skin of that barren sort' and some of the most entertaining moments of the play depend on his shameless, boastful antics. Yet he also has contrastingly heroic qualities of enthusiasm, self-belief and openness to experience which we have to admire.

Immediate focus on task and key words and example from text

2. USE OF TITLES, NAMES, ETC.

This is a simple, but important, tip to stay on the right side of the examiners.

- Make sure that you spell correctly the titles of the texts, chapters, name of authors and so on. Present them correctly, too, with double quotation marks and capitals as appropriate. For example, '*In Scene 1 of "A Midsummer Night's Dream" …*'
- Use the **full title**, unless there is a good reason not to (e.g. it's very long).
- Use the terms 'play' or 'text' rather than 'book' or 'story'. If you use the word 'story', the examiner may think you mean the plot/action rather than the 'text' as a whole.

3. EFFECTIVE QUOTATIONS

Do not 'bolt on' quotations to the points you make. You will get some marks for including them, but examiners will not find your writing very fluent.

The best quotations are:

- Relevant
- Not too long
- Integrated into your argument/sentence.

TARGETING A HIGH GRADE   A01

Here is an example of a quotation successfully embedded in a sentence:

Coming after the lovers' confusion, Bottom's homely comment that 'reason and love keep little company together' shows his underlying common sense.

Remember – quotations can be a well-selected set of three or four single words or phrases. These can be easily embedded into a sentence to build a picture or explanation around your point. Or, they can be longer quotations that are explored and picked apart.

4. TECHNIQUES AND TERMINOLOGY

By all means mention literary terms, techniques, conventions or people (for example, **dramatic irony** or 'Apuleius') **but** make sure that you:

- Understand what they mean
- Are able to link them to what you're saying
- Spell them correctly.

5. GENERAL WRITING SKILLS

Try to write in a way that sounds professional and uses standard English. This does not mean that your writing will lack personality – just that it will be authoritative.

- Avoid colloquial or everyday expressions such as 'got', 'alright', 'ok' and so on.
- Use terms such as 'convey', 'suggest', 'imply', 'infer' to explain the writer's methods.
- Refer to 'we' when discussing the audience/reader.
- Avoid assertions and generalisations; don't just state a general point of view (*Egeus's attitude is cruel and villainous*), but analyse closely, with clear evidence and textual detail.

TARGETING A HIGH GRADE   A01

Note the professional approach in this example:

Egeus is a stock character of comedy, the self-righteous father determined to thwart his daughter in her choice of a husband. Although he threatens to have Hermia executed, the nagging tone and exaggerated complaints which accompany his threat imply that Egeus is merely blustering. The power of execution is in the hands of Theseus, a far more sensible figure, and from this we can infer that, despite Egeus's bullying, Hermia is unlikely to perish.

GRADE BOOSTER A02

It is important to remember that *A Midsummer Night's Dream* is a text created by Shakespeare – thinking about the choices Shakespeare makes with language and plotting will not only alert you to his methods as a playwright, but also his intentions, i.e. the effect he seeks to create.

QUESTIONS WITH STATEMENTS, QUOTATIONS OR VIEWPOINTS

One type of question you may come across includes a statement, quotation or viewpoint from another reader.

These questions ask you to respond to, or argue for/against, a specific point of view or critical interpretation.

For *A Midsummer Night's Dream* these questions will typically be like this:

- **Discuss the view that *A Midsummer Night's Dream* is not one play but an unsatisfactory combination of three.**
- **How far do you agree that the play endorses male superiority?**
- **To what extent do you agree that the contrast between the two settings, Athens and the wood, is central to the meaning of the play?**
- **'The course of true love never did run smooth.' Explore the degree to which this theme is developed in the course of the play.**

The key thing to remember is that you are being asked to **respond to a critical interpretation** of the text – in other words, to come up with **your own 'take'** on the idea or viewpoint in the task.

KEY SKILLS REQUIRED

The table below provides help and advice on answering this type of question:

SKILL	MEANS?	HOW DO I ACHIEVE THIS?
Consider different interpretations	There will be more than one way of looking at the given question. For example, critics might be divided about the extent of the play's structural unity.	• Show you have considered these different interpretations in your answer. For example: *It is true that the lovers, the fairies and the craftsmen give us distinct types of entertainment. Past productions have even cut or reordered them to prioritise one over another. However, the fairies and the craftsmen come into the play because of their relevance to the story of the lovers and a careful reading will show how they complement and illuminate it.*
Write with a clear, personal voice	Your own 'take' on the question is made obvious to the marker. You are not just repeating other people's ideas, but offering what **you** think.	• Although you may mention different perspectives on the task, you settle on your own view. • Use language that shows careful, but confident, consideration. For example: *Although it has been said that … I feel that …*
Construct a coherent argument	The examiner or marker can follow your train of thought so that your own viewpoint is clear to him or her.	• Write in clear paragraphs that deal logically with different aspects of the question. • Support what you say with well-selected and relevant evidence. • Use a range of connectives to help 'signpost' your argument. For example: **In one respect**, the events in the wood are the stuff of nightmares. **In another**, they are a source of joy. The two aspects are, **moreover**, inextricably linked.

ANSWERING A 'VIEWPOINT' QUESTION

Here is an example of a typical question on *A Midsummer Night's Dream*:

Discuss the view that *A Midsummer Night's Dream* is not one play but an unsatisfactory combination of three.

STAGE 1: DECODE THE QUESTION

Underline/highlight the **key words**, and make sure you understand what the statement, quotation or viewpoint is saying. In this case:

Key words = Discuss/unsatisfactory/combination/three

The viewpoint/idea expressed is = the play contains three stories which do not achieve a unity

STAGE 2: DECIDE WHAT YOUR VIEWPOINT IS

Examiners have stated that they tend to reward a strong view which is clearly put. Think about the question – can you take issue with it? Disagreeing strongly can lead to higher marks, provided you have **genuine evidence** to support your point of view. Don't disagree just for the sake of it.

STAGE 3: DECIDE HOW TO STRUCTURE YOUR ANSWER

Pick out the key points you wish to make, and decide on the order in which you will present them. Keep this basic plan to hand while you write your response.

STAGE 4: WRITE YOUR RESPONSE

You could start by expanding on the statement or viewpoint expressed in the question.

- For example, in **paragraph 1**:

"A Midsummer Night's Dream" tells a story about four young lovers, but they have to compete for our attention with fairies who magically assist them, and with amateur actors who overcome daunting obstacles to entertain them. Each group makes for a tale on its own.

This could help by setting up the various ideas you will choose to explore, argue for/ against, and so on. But do not just repeat what the question says or just say what you are going to do. Get straight to the point. For example:

We should not, however, assume, that these three sub-plots will distract from each other. On the contrary, as they interact, each may add to the others' dramatic effectiveness and offer a complementary treatment of the play's themes.

Then, proceed to set out the different arguments or critical perspectives, including your own. This might be done by dealing with specific aspects or elements of the play, one by one. Consider giving 1–2 paragraphs to explore each aspect in turn. Discuss the strengths and weaknesses in each particular point of view. For example:

- **Paragraph 2**: first aspect:

*To answer whether this interpretation is valid, we need to **first of all** look at …*

*It is clear from this that… /a **strength** of this argument is …*

*However, I believe this suggests that …/a **weakness** in this argument is …*

- **Paragraph 3**: a new focus or aspect:

Turning our attention to the critical idea that … it could be said that …

- **Paragraphs 4, 5, etc. onwards**: develop the argument, building a convincing set of points:

Furthermore, if we look at …

- **Last paragraph**: end with a clear statement of your view, without simply listing all the points you have made:

*To say that the play combines three separate stories is misleading, as **I believe that** …*

> **EXAMINER'S TIP** ✓
>
> You should comment concisely, professionally and thoughtfully and present a range of viewpoints. Try using modal verbs such as 'could', 'might', 'may' to clarify your own interpretation. For additional help on **Using critical interpretations and perspectives,** see pages 90 and 91.

> **EXAMINER'S TIP** ✓
>
> Note how the ideas are clearly signposted through a range of connectives and linking phrases, such as 'However' and 'Turning our attention to …'

COMPARING *A MIDSUMMER NIGHT'S DREAM* WITH OTHER TEXTS

As part of your assessment, you may have to compare *A Midsummer Night's Dream* with, or link it to, other texts that you have studied. These may be other plays, novels or even poetry. You may also have to link or draw in references from texts written by critics. For example:

> **Compare the dramatic techniques writers employ to produce comedy in *A Midsummer Night's Dream* and other text(s) you have studied.**

THE TASK

Your task is likely to be on a method, issue, viewpoint or key aspect that is common to *A Midsummer Night's Dream* and the other text(s), so you will need to:

Evaluate the issue or statement and have an **open-minded approach**. The best answers suggest meaning**s** and interpretation**s** (plural):

- What do you understand by the question? Is this theme more important in one text than in another? Why? How? What do you understand by the term anyway?
- What are the different ways that this question or aspect can be read or viewed?
- Can you challenge the viewpoint, if there is one? If so, what evidence is there? How can you present it in a thoughtful, reflective way?

Express **original or creative approaches** fluently:

- This isn't about coming up with entirely new ideas, but you need to show that you're actively engaged with thinking about the question, not just reproducing random facts and information you have learned.
- **Synthesise** your ideas – pull ideas and points together to create something fresh.
- This is a linking/comparison response, so ensure that you guide your reader through your ideas logically, clearly and with professional language.

Know **what to compare/contrast**: **form, structure** and **language** will **always** be central to your response, even where you also have to write about characters, contexts or culture.

- Think about standard versus more conventional narration (for example, use of **soliloquies, foreshadowing**, parallel characters, comic behaviour and **dramatic irony**).
- Consider different characteristic uses of language: lengths of lines, use of formal and informal styles, **verse** and **prose**, direct address to the audience.
- Look at a variety of **symbols, images**, motifs (how they represent concerns of author/time; what they are and how and where they appear; how they link to critical perspectives; their purposes, effects and impact on the play).
- Consider aspects of **genres** (to what extent do Shakespeare and the author(s) of the other work(s) conform to/challenge/subvert particular genres or styles of writing such as courtly love and high **tragedy**).

EXAMINER'S TIP ✓

Be sure to give due weight to each text – if there are two texts, this would normally mean giving them equal attention (but check the exact requirements of your task). Where required or suggested by the course you are following, you could try moving fluently between the texts in each paragraph, as an alternative to treating texts separately. This approach can be impressive and will ensure that comparison is central to your response.

WRITING YOUR RESPONSE

The depth and extent of your answer will depend on how much you have to write, but the key will be to **explore in detail**, and **link between ideas and texts**. Let us use the same example:

> **Compare the dramatic techniques writers employ to produce comedy in *A Midsummer Night's Dream* and other text(s) you have studied.**

INTRODUCTION TO YOUR RESPONSE

- Briefly discuss what 'dramatic techniques' means, and how well this applies to your texts.
- Mention in support the importance of specific dramatic techniques in *A Midsummmer Night's Dream* and the other text(s).
- You could begin with a powerful quotation that you use to launch into your response. For example:

> *'Churl, upon thy eyes I throw / All the power this charm doth owe,' boasts the puck, convinced that he has Demetrius in his power. In "Love's Labour's Lost" Berowne is equally confident as he emerges from hiding to denounce his lovelorn colleagues. The audience, however, already sees the dramatic irony that will shortly overtake them.*

MAIN BODY OF YOUR RESPONSE

- **Point 1**: start with the use of dramatic irony in *A Midsummer Night's Dream* and what it tells us about the play's concerns. What is your view? Are the uses of dramatic irony similar in the other text(s)? Are there any relevant critical viewpoints that you know about? Are there contextual or cultural factors to consider?

- **Point 2**: now cover a new treatment or aspect through comparison or contrast of this theme in your other text(s). How is this treatment or aspect presented **differently or similarly** by the writer(s) in the language, form, structures used? Why was this done in this way? How does it reflect the writers' interests? What do the critics say? Are there contextual or cultural factors to consider?

- **Points 3, 4, 5, etc.**: address a range of other factors and aspects, for example the use of mistaken language **either** within *A Midsummer Night's Dream* **or** in both *A Midsummer Night's Dream* and another text. What different ways do you respond to these (with more empathy, greater criticism, less interest) – and why? For example:

> *We are amused when Bottom urges his colleagues to rehearse 'obscenely', while Costard from "Love Labour's Lost" thinks that 'remuneration' and 'guerdon' are the names of coins – yet their ignorance does not detract from their charm and energy.*

CONCLUSION

- Synthesise elements of what you have said into a final paragraph that fluently, succinctly and inventively leaves the reader/examiner with the sense that you have engaged with this task and the texts. For example:

> *In both plays Shakespeare creates absurd predicaments which the characters attempt to negotiate with little success, their folly shown by dramatic irony and by their misuse of language. In one case, supernatural intervention by fairies helps to solve their problems; in the other, the happy ending is glimpsed but has to be postponed due to a death.*

EXAMINER'S TIP

Be creative with your conclusion! It's the last thing the examiner will read and your chance to make your mark.

RESPONDING TO A GENERAL QUESTION ABOUT THE WHOLE TEXT

You may also be asked to write about a specific aspect of *A Midsummer Night's Dream* – but as it relates to the **whole text**. For example:

> **Explore the dramatic use Shakespeare makes of supernatural and imaginative elements in *A Midsummer Night's Dream*.**

This means you should:

- Focus on *both* **the supernatural** *and* **the imaginative specifically** (not the fantastic in general).
- **Explain their 'dramatic use'– how** they are used by Shakespeare in terms of action, character and furthering ideas or themes. Consider the dramatic conventions linked to them – the appearance of fairies, the associations of night and dreams, the **parody** element of the play within the play.
- Look at aspects of the **whole play text**, not just one scene.

STRUCTURING YOUR RESPONSE

You need a clear, logical plan, as for all tasks that you do. It is impossible to write about every section or part of the text, so you will need to:

- Quickly note 5–6 key points or aspects to build your essay around, e.g.

  Point a *the fairies' actions highlight aspects of love*

  Point b *'Pyramus and Thisbe' encourages us to think about how drama works*

  Point c *it is ironic that Theseus dismisses the imagination as a delusion*

  Point d *the fairies introduce entertaining dramatic effects*

  Point e *there is a contrast between daytime rationality and night-time fantasy*

- Then decide the most effective or logical order. For example, **point c**, then **e**, **d**, **a**, **b**, etc.

You could begin with your key or main idea, with supporting evidence/references, followed by your further points (perhaps two paragraphs for each). For example:

Paragraph 1: first key point: *Theseus's dismissal of 'antique fables' and 'imagination' is deeply ironic since he is himself a character from ancient myth appearing in a work of the imagination. His words challenge us to find a more positive view of what he condemns.*

Paragraph 2: expand out, link into other areas: *Shakespeare does not require us to believe in fairies literally, but we do have to accept their supernatural deeds as part of the play, just as we accept the existence of the earthbound craftsmen.*

Paragraph 3: change direction, introduce new aspect/point: *The Athenians seem to need their dream-like night in the wood, perhaps implying we all need imagination in our lives.*

And so on.

- **For your conclusion**, use a compelling way to finish, perhaps repeating some or all of the key words from the question. For example, either:

End with your final point, but **add a last clause** which makes it clear what you think is key to the question: e.g. *Shakespeare's inclusion of the supernatural and imaginative elements of the play not only add to its dramatic power, but draw attention to the nature of drama itself, which enhances and transforms reality in order to give us a new perspective.* Or:

End with a **new quotation** or **an aspect that's slightly different from** your main point: e.g. *In his concluding speech, Shakespeare may seem to be implying through the puck that the play with its 'weak and idle theme' can offer us no more than can 'a dream', but the function of dreams remains an intriguing mystery to this day and so does the power of imagination.* Or, of course, you can combine these endings.

EXAMINER'S TIP ✓

You may be asked to discuss other texts you have studied as well as *A Midsummer Night's Dream* as part of your response. Once you have completed your response on the play you could move on to discuss the same issues in your other text(s). Begin with a simple linking phrase or sentence to launch straight into your first point about your next text, such as: *The supernatural is presented in a quite different way in "The Tempest". Here, …*

WRITING ABOUT CONTEXTS

Assessment Objective 4 asks you to 'demonstrate understanding of the significance and influence of the contexts in which literary texts are written and received ...' This can mean:

- How the events, settings, politics and so on **of the time when the text was written** influenced the writer or help us to understand the play's themes or concerns. For example, to what extent might Shakespeare's depiction of the craftsmen reflect Elizabethan actors' need for aristocratic patronage?

or

- How events, settings, politics and so on **of the time when the text is read or seen** influences how it is understood. For example, would audiences watching the play today respond differently to the presentation of male authority over women than Shakespeare's original audience?

THE CONTEXT FOR *A MIDSUMMER NIGHT'S DREAM*

You might find the following table of suggested examples helpful for thinking about how particular aspects of the time contribute to our understanding of the play and its themes. These are just examples – can you think of any others?

POLITICAL	LITERARY	PHILOSOPHICAL
Elizabeth I, a female monarch in a patriarchal society	Elizabethan romances, Ovid	Ancient Athens, famed for its rational thinkers

SCIENTIFIC	CULTURAL	SOCIAL
Dreams as revelations	Fairy folklore, May Day celebrations	Attitudes to social groups: aristocrats, workmen …

> **EXAMINER'S TIP**
>
> Remember that linking the historical, literary or social context to the play is key to achieving the best marks for AO4.

TARGETING A HIGH GRADE (AO4)

Remember that the extent to which you write about these contexts will be determined by the marks available. Some questions or tasks may have very few marks allocated for **AO4**, but where you do have to refer to context the key thing is **not** to 'bolt on' your comments, or write a long, separate chunk of text on context and then 'go back' to the play. For example:

Don't just write:

A puck is a kind of goblin. The word derives from 'pook', a name for the devil which appears in William Langland's "Piers Plowman" and Edmund Spenser's "Epithalamion". The puck featured in the play is one named Robin Goodfellow, though he also answers to the name of 'Hobgoblin'. Country folk called him 'Goodfellow' in order to flatter him, in hopes that he would leave them alone. Before Shakespeare's play, Robin Goodfellow was not usually classed as a puck, but as an earth spirit. He always carried a broom with him, so that he could help maids who had earned his assistance by their good behaviour. More often, however, he liked to cause mischief, like souring milk or butter in the churn.

Do write:

Robin Goodfellow is a well-known figure from folklore, a mischievous goblin or 'puck' who likes to disrupt housework, but who may also help deserving maids. Shakespeare does not rely on the audience knowing about the puck, since the folk old tales were inconsistent with one another and gradually dying out. Instead, on his first appearance, Robin discusses his characteristics with a fairy and so quickly establishes his credentials as a prankster. Later in the scene we see him in the role of Oberon's loyal assistant, but we have already heard enough about his love of mischief to expect that he will soon be perpetrating outrageous practical jokes.

USING CRITICAL INTERPRETATIONS AND PERSPECTIVES

THE 'MEANING' OF A TEXT

There are many viewpoints and perspectives on the 'meaning' of *A Midsummer Night's Dream*, and examiners will be looking for evidence that you have considered a range of these. Broadly speaking, these different interpretations might relate to the following considerations:

1. CHARACTER

What **sort/type** of person Bottom – or another character – is:

- Is the character an 'archetype' (a specific type of character with common features)? Harold Bloom describes Bottom as a 'wise clown', someone whom we can laugh at yet we may also laugh with. In this, he might be compared with later figures from Don Quixote to Huckleberry Finn, or even Homer Simpson.
- Does the character **personify**, **symbolise** or represent a specific idea or trope? (For example, a passionate desire to excel which is let down by an utter lack of talent.)
- Is the character modern, universal, of his/her time, historically accurate, etc? Is Bottom compatible with the many weavers who protested about prices and unemployment in this period? Are there ordinary working people with similar flair and resilience in our own time?

2. IDEAS AND ISSUES

What the play tells us about **particular ideas or issues** and how we can interpret these. For example:

- The nature of theatre
- The roles of men and women in Elizabethan society and within marriage
- What comedy means
- Moral and social codes, etc.

3. LINKS AND CONTEXTS

To what extent the play **links with, follows or pre-echoes** other texts and/or ideas. For example:

- Its influence culturally, historically and socially (do we see echoes of the characters or **genres** in other texts?) How like the puck are comedians like Charlie Chaplin, and why? Does the play share features with, for example, West End farces?
- How its language links to other texts or modes, such as religious works, myth, legend, etc.

4. DRAMATIC STRUCTURE

How the play is **constructed** and how Shakespeare **makes** his narrative:

- Does it follow a particular dramatic convention?
- What is the function of specific events, characters, theatrical devices, staging, etc. in relation to narrative?
- What are the specific moments of tension, conflict, crisis and denouement – and do we agree on what they are?

CRITICAL VIEWPOINT A03

Bottom is usually interpreted as a positive figure, but Sophie Gilbert praises Bruce's Dow's 'brilliantly effective' performance as an 'utterly obnoxious' Bottom, hiding the character's comic ignorance under a layer of diva-like petulance and absurd self-satisfaction' (a 2012 performance by the Shakespeare Theatre Company, reviewed in the *Washingtonian*.)

CRITICAL VIEWPOINT A03

'Tommy Aslett simply roars around the stage as Bottom in a masterclass of slapstick vigour, the audience convulsing with laughter at his well-meaning buffoonery. The physicality of the production is phenomenal ... ' (Matt Fancy in *The Stage* on a 2013 production by the Sell a Door theatre company.)

5. AUDIENCE RESPONSE

How the play **works on an audience**, and whether this changes over time and in different contexts:

● Are we to empathise with, feel distance from, judge and/or evaluate the events and characters?

6. CRITICAL REACTION

And finally, how different audiences view the play. For example:

● Different **theatre critics over time**
● Different **audiences** in **earlier or more recent years** (see **Part Five: Critical debates**).

WRITING ABOUT CRITICAL PERSPECTIVES

The important thing to remember is that **you** are a critic, too. Your job is to evaluate what a critic or school of criticism has said about the elements above, and arrive at your own conclusions.

In essence, you need to: **consider** the views of others, **synthesise** them, then decide on **your perspective**. For example:

EXPLAIN THE VIEWPOINTS:

Critical view A about how we evaluate Theseus:

> *Peter Hollindale judges that Theseus functions as the voice of reason. He is 'a most impressive order-figure … a benevolent offstage protector of those entangled in anarchic comedy', even though Theseus's appreciation of the imagination may be limited.*

Critical view B about how we evaluate Theseus:

> *To Shirley Nelson Garner, Theseus is notable as a figure of patriarchal authority who is 'unsympathetic toward women'. He overrules Egeus only after he has had the satisfaction of conquering and possessing Hippolyta.*

THEN SYNTHESISE AND ADD YOUR PERSPECTIVE:

Synthesising these views whilst adding your own:

> *Theseus is a powerful figure in the mortal world and, as Peter Hollindale points out, he uses his position to help others and maintain order. However, Theseus has limitations. While Hollindale notes his inability to appreciate the imagination, Shirley Nelson Garner points to the repressive patriarchal attitude evident in his initial response to Hermia and, we might add, shared by his equivalent in the fairy world, Oberon. These limitations are important, but they do not in my view make Theseus a bad ruler since everyone's point of view is limited. Perhaps Shakespeare is hinting that even the greatest of us needs to open his mind through poetry and drama.*

GRADE BOOSTER **A03**

Make sure you have thoroughly explored the dramatic conventions (some of which – such as **soliloquy** – are mentioned above). Critical interpretation of drama is different from critical interpretation of other modes of writing – not least because of audience response, and the specific theatrical devices in use. Key critics are theatre critics – look at what they have to say about recent productions. Two comments on recent productions are given on the opposite page.

ANNOTATED SAMPLE ANSWERS

Below are extracts from two sample answers to the same question at different grades. Bear in mind that these are examples only, covering all four Assessment Objectives – you will need to check the type of question and the weightings given for the four Assessment Objectives when writing your coursework essay or practising for your exam.

> Question: **How important are the magical elements of the play to its success thematically and dramatically?**

CANDIDATE 1

This is part of a longer response of 1,200 words.

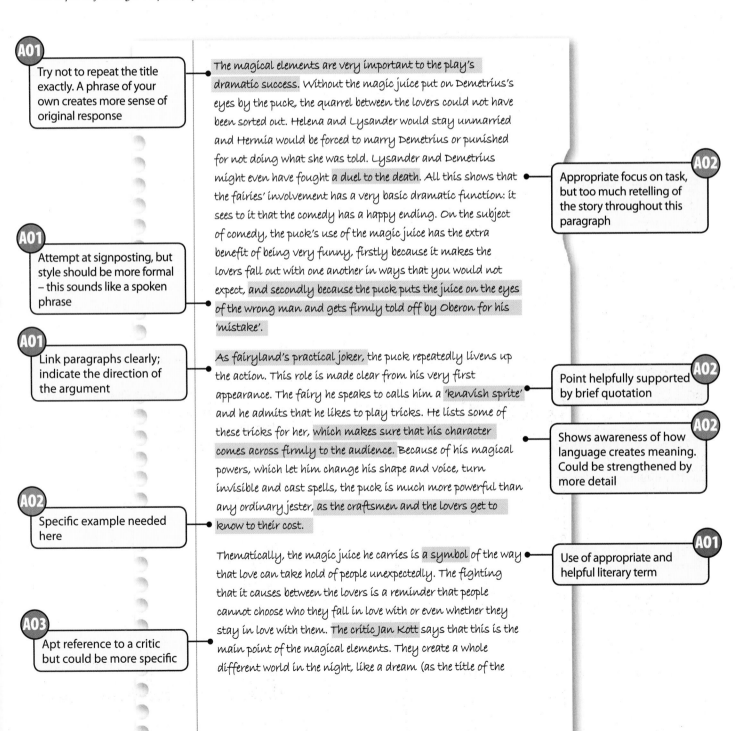

AO1
Try not to repeat the title exactly. A phrase of your own creates more sense of original response

AO1
Attempt at signposting, but style should be more formal – this sounds like a spoken phrase

AO1
Link paragraphs clearly; indicate the direction of the argument

AO2
Specific example needed here

AO3
Apt reference to a critic but could be more specific

The magical elements are very important to the play's dramatic success. Without the magic juice put on Demetrius's eyes by the puck, the quarrel between the lovers could not have been sorted out. Helena and Lysander would stay unmarried and Hermia would be forced to marry Demetrius or punished for not doing what she was told. Lysander and Demetrius might even have fought a duel to the death. All this shows that the fairies' involvement has a very basic dramatic function: it sees to it that the comedy has a happy ending. On the subject of comedy, the puck's use of the magic juice has the extra benefit of being very funny, firstly because it makes the lovers fall out with one another in ways that you would not expect, and secondly because the puck puts the juice on the eyes of the wrong man and gets firmly told off by Oberon for his 'mistake'.

As fairyland's practical joker, the puck repeatedly livens up the action. This role is made clear from his very first appearance. The fairy he speaks to calls him a 'knavish sprite' and he admits that he likes to play tricks. He lists some of these tricks for her, which makes sure that his character comes across firmly to the audience. Because of his magical powers, which let him change his shape and voice, turn invisible and cast spells, the puck is much more powerful than any ordinary jester, as the craftsmen and the lovers get to know to their cost.

Thematically, the magic juice he carries is a symbol of the way that love can take hold of people unexpectedly. The fighting that it causes between the lovers is a reminder that people cannot choose who they fall in love with or even whether they stay in love with them. The critic Jan Kott says that this is the main point of the magical elements. They create a whole different world in the night, like a dream (as the title of the

AO2
Appropriate focus on task, but too much retelling of the story throughout this paragraph

AO2
Point helpfully supported by brief quotation

AO2
Shows awareness of how language creates meaning. Could be strengthened by more detail

AO1
Use of appropriate and helpful literary term

A04
Add context that the critic is influenced by Freud's theories of dreams

A02
The quotation requires context and analysis and should be embedded

A04
Clear reference to how the drama works on stage

A01
Use of brackets to link to question title is clumsy. Should be put into a separate sentence

play tells us), where the characters' deep, forbidden desires can be expressed. Of course, this aspect of the play is most effective when the actors' parts are doubled. At the start of the play Hippolyta sounds reluctant to marry Theseus ('Four days will quickly steep themselves in night'), but in the wood at night her magic self, Titania, can be much more independent and defy her magic partner, Oberon.

Kott claims that Titania's involvement with Bottom shows her secret longing for 'animal love', but this has to be taking the argument too far. Bottom has not really been turned into an animal, only been given the head of an ass, which has the effect of making him look ridiculous and stupid. Once again, the magical element sets up a comic situation, but it also allows Bottom a chance to show how well he can cope (which is dramatically important in building his character) and mocks the class divisions which make the royals and the commoners seem like different species (a thematic contribution).

A03
Shows awareness of alternative ways of staging, but is too vague – which actors? which parts?

A03
Comments critically on an interpretation and supports point with evidence

A04
Successfully brings in social, political context

GRADE C

The remainder of the essay considers how each mortal's response to the magic elements helps to define their character and ends with a consideration of how the fairies' singing and dancing adds to the play's effectiveness, especially at its conclusion.

Comment

A01 Expression, though sometimes lacking fluency, is mostly clear. The material covered is relevant, but there is a tendency towards narrative description of events, and the relevance of these to the question is not always made sufficiently clear. Signposting needs to be firmer and more formal. A topic sentence for each paragraph would give a greater sense of direction.

A02 There is a sustained response to the magical elements of the play, with due attention paid to their thematic significance and dramatic development. Knowledge of structure and dramatic effect is good, but the points made are not regularly supported by quotation and analysis. The comments on language are mostly implicit and there is no detailed textual commentary.

A03 There is some consideration of alternative interpretations of Bottom's transformation and some awareness that the play can be staged in more than one way. Both points could be developed in more detail.

A04 Contextual references are brief but effective.

For a B grade
To gain a higher grade, the answer would need to include at least some of the following:

- Tighter focus on the argument, less retelling of the story.
- More detailed, evaluative accounts of examples, including dramatic effects and language.
- Different interpretations developed in more depth.

CANDIDATE 2

This is part of a longer response of 1,200 words

A02

Shows grasp of structure and establishes its relevance to the question

A04

Historical context helpfully introduced

A02

Excellent comparison

Although "A Midsummer Night's Dream" begins and ends at the Athenian court, most of the play (Acts II to IV) takes place in a wood beyond the city, where invisible fairies cast spells over two groups of humans. In the short term, the spells produce chaos and dramatic conflict, which is entertaining for the audience, but stressful for the characters. In the longer term, the humans' problems are solved and, along the way, the audience are encouraged to see the irrationality of love, theatre and social hierarchy. The interaction between the magical fairies and the Athenian mortals therefore strongly shapes the play's dramatic power and meaning.

Athens is a city famous for its great philosophers like Aristotle, so it is only to be expected that its ruler, Duke Theseus, is a man of reason, maintaining order and promoting reconciliation. When Hermia refuses her father's choice of husband, Theseus feels obliged to take a firm line with her, but his reference to 'some private schooling' lets us know that he is going to have equally firm words with Egeus and Demetrius to persuade them to climb down. Theseus is proud of his emotional intelligence, boasting to Hippolyta of his success in dealing with nervous dignitaries, but the evidence suggests that he is less skilled than he thinks. He allows demoralising comments about the craftsmen's play to be heard by them, he fails to get Hippolyta enthusiastic about their wedding, and his reasoning never persuades anyone to change their mind about anything. It takes the magical intervention of the fairies, not the arguments of Theseus, to put Demetrius back in touch with his true feelings.

The world of the fairies is a kind of alternative world to Theseus's court, a chaotic place where the problems of love can be explored with greater dramatic effect. The fairy king and queen are a similarly troubled couple to Theseus and Hippolyta, but they express themselves more passionately – they make wild allegations and enlist their supporters against each other. Where Theseus tries to play down his military conquest of Hippolyta, Oberon is more than ready to humiliate and subdue his wife, putting the juice on her eyes with the curse, 'Wake when something vile is near!'. Many productions have brought out the link by casting the same two actors as the couples. Some also use the actors playing Bottom's fellow craftsmen as his fairy attendants. These doublings are likely to be effective in entertaining the audience. They turn Theseus into a vengeful supernatural force and Quince into a grovelling servant, which is bound to seem comical.

A01

Argument clearly related to the question

A01

Points supported by examples drawn from different parts of the play

A01

Brings it back to the question

A03

Notes how the text has been interpreted

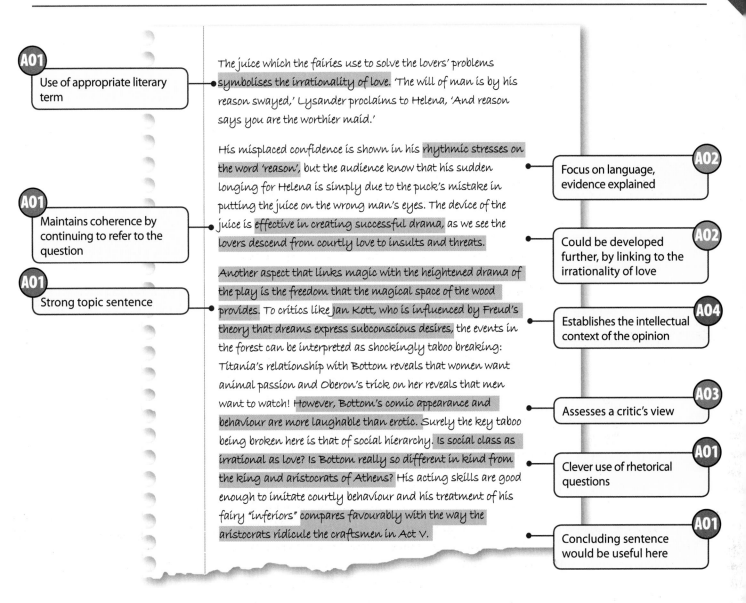

AO1 Use of appropriate literary term

AO1 Maintains coherence by continuing to refer to the question

AO1 Strong topic sentence

The juice which the fairies use to solve the lovers' problems symbolises the irrationality of love. 'The will of man is by his reason swayed,' Lysander proclaims to Helena, 'And reason says you are the worthier maid.'

His misplaced confidence is shown in his rhythmic stresses on the word 'reason', but the audience know that his sudden longing for Helena is simply due to the puck's mistake in putting the juice on the wrong man's eyes. The device of the juice is effective in creating successful drama, as we see the lovers descend from courtly love to insults and threats.

Another aspect that links magic with the heightened drama of the play is the freedom that the magical space of the wood provides. To critics like Jan Kott, who is influenced by Freud's theory that dreams express subconscious desires, the events in the forest can be interpreted as shockingly taboo breaking: Titania's relationship with Bottom reveals that women want animal passion and Oberon's trick on her reveals that men want to watch! However, Bottom's comic appearance and behaviour are more laughable than erotic. Surely the key taboo being broken here is that of social hierarchy. Is social class as irrational as love? Is Bottom really so different in kind from the king and aristocrats of Athens? His acting skills are good enough to imitate courtly behaviour and his treatment of his fairy "inferiors" compares favourably with the way the aristocrats ridicule the craftsmen in Act V.

AO2 Focus on language, evidence explained

AO2 Could be developed further, by linking to the irrationality of love

AO4 Establishes the intellectual context of the opinion

AO3 Assesses a critic's view

AO1 Clever use of rhetorical questions

AO1 Concluding sentence would be useful here

The remainder of the essay considers how, as the action moves back to Athens and the daytime, a calm, rational view of love, art and the social order is reinstated by Theseus, and the comedy comes to a satisfying conclusion. However, significant reminders of human nature's irrationality remain, not least the return of the fairies and the puck's reminder to the audience that they have chosen to watch actors pretending to be supernatural beings.

Comment

AO1 There is a clear sense from the opening that the candidate has a grasp of the whole play and of the question. The answer is shaped by an overview which links together incidents throughout the play and each paragraph moves the argument forward. Writing is generally fluent with appropriate critical vocabulary.

AO2 Examples of structure, form and language are used to support the argument. Quotations are neatly integrated into the discussion and supported by analytical comments.

AO3 The candidate is aware that production choices, such as doubling parts, will affect interpretation. Alternative interpretations of Bottom's transformation are not only considered, but used as the basis to introduce a further interpretation.

AO4 The question is illuminated by a number of contextual references, covering both the text and how it has been interpreted.

For an A* grade

- A sense of how the play was received at the time when it was first performed would enrich the comments on its dramatic success.
- At times, ideas could be elaborated on and taken a stage further – paragraphs begin in a very focused way but do not always finish as strongly.
- A counter-argument could be touched upon.

WORKING THROUGH A TASK

Now it's your turn to work through a task on *A Midsummer Night's Dream*. The key is to:

- Read/decode the task/question
- Plan your points – then expand and link your points
- Draft your answer.

TASK TITLE

> **How far do you agree that Shakespeare portrays Bottom as an admirable character rather than a fool?**

DECODE THE QUESTION: KEY WORDS

How far do you agree..?	= what are **my** views?
Shakespeare portrays	= a reminder that this is a literary creation
admirable character	= a character with positive qualities
fool	= one whose foolishness makes him laughable

PLAN AND EXPAND

- Key aspect: evidence of 'admirable character'

POINT	EXPANDED POINT	EVIDENCE
Point a Bottom brings enormous enthusiasm to the craftsmen's play	Bottom lacks talent and judgement, but is so keen that he offers to play all of the parts himself. He energises the other craftsmen and he puts forward solutions for any problems.	'Let me play the lion too' (I.2.57) 'I have a device to make all well' (III.1.13)
Point b He responds positively to his transformation and encounter with Titania	Different aspects of this point expanded *You fill in*	Quotations 1–2 *You fill in*
Point c He is not intimidated by the aristocratic audience in Act V	Different aspects of this point expanded *You fill in*	Quotations 1–2 *You fill in*

- Key aspect: evidence of 'fool'

POINT	EXPANDED POINT	EVIDENCE
Point a *You fill in*	Expanded: *You fill in*	Quotations 1–2 *You fill in*
Point b *You fill in*	Different aspects of this point expanded *You fill in*	Quotations 1–2 *You fill in*
Point c *You fill in*	Different aspects of this point expanded *You fill in*	Quotations 1–2 *You fill in*

CONCLUSION

POINT	EXPANDED POINT	EVIDENCE
Key final point or overall view *You fill in*	Draw together and perhaps add a final further point to support your view *You fill in*	Final quotation to support your view *You fill in*

DEVELOP FURTHER, THEN DRAFT

Now look back over your draft points and:

● Add further links or connections between the points to develop them further or synthesise what has been said, for example:

> *Peter Hollindale points out that Bottom's shortcomings – his 'complacency and self-centredness … his lack of imagination and defective acting' – equip him to cope with the supernatural challenge of the wood more constructively than the lovers. It is at this point in the play that we begin to laugh with Bottom rather than at him, yet the key reason we enjoy his triumph is that we know underneath it he remains an insensitive fool.*

● Decide an order for your points/paragraphs – some may now be linked/connected and therefore **not** in the order of the table above.

● Now draft your essay. If you're really stuck you can use the opening paragraph below to get you started.

> *The puck uses his supernatural insight to single out Bottom from the other craftsmen as 'The shallowest thick-skin of that barren sort' (III.2.13). When Bottom performs as Pyramus, Demetrius judges that he fails to act like a man, let alone a hero. Yet, if we were to rank all the characters in the play by how much we admire them, there would be a good case to give the top position to the weaver whose friends declare that he has 'the best wit of any handicraft man in Athens' (IV.2.7) ….*

Once you've written your essay, turn to page 104 for a mark scheme on this question to see how well you've done.

FURTHER QUESTIONS

1. Explore the ways in which comedy is created in *A Midsummer Night's Dream*.

2. To what extent are *A Midsummer Night's Dream* and another comedy you have studied about the successful resolution of conflicts?

3. What would be lost if the craftsmen's scenes were to be removed from *A Midsummer Night's Dream*?

4. 'The female characters in *A Midsummer Night's Dream* are easily and naturally subdued.' Discuss.

5. According to William Hazlitt, '*A Midsummer Night's Dream*, when acted, is converted from a delightful fiction into a dull pantomime'. Discuss how far you agree with this view, with reference to one or more productions you have seen.

6. Does *A Midsummer Night's Dream* celebrate or ridicule love? How does the treatment of love differ in *Twelfth Night*?

7. To what extent do you agree that *A Midsummer Night's Dream* is not a play about individual characters, but about the relationship between them?

8. Elliot Krieger argues that the play reinforces social hierarchy, confirming Theseus as the ultimate figure of authority. To what extent do you agree with this view?

9. A friend has asked you for advice on how the part of Oberon should be played. Write a letter discussing the question, with particular reference to Act III Scene 2.

ESSENTIAL STUDY TOOLS

FURTHER READING

EDITIONS OF THE TEXT

R. A. Foakes, ed., *A Midsummer Night's Dream*, The New Cambridge Shakespeare, Cambridge University Press, 2003
   The edition of the text used in the preparation of these Notes; has a useful introduction to the play which includes a stage history and an account of Shakespeare's sources

Harold F. Brooks, ed., *A Midsummer Night's Dream*, The Arden Shakespeare, Nelson, Walton-on-Thames, 1997
   A scholarly edition with a thorough introduction and extracts from source materials

Trevor R. Griffiths, ed., *A Midsummer Night's Dream*, Shakespeare in Production, Cambridge University Press, 1996
   An edition which gives details of how the play has been performed in past productions, explained through an introduction and a commentary running beneath the text

CRITICISM

CONTEMPORARY CRITICISM

Catherine Belsey, *Why Shakespeare?*, Palgrave Macmillan, London, 2007
   Examines how Shakespeare uses material from folk tales, with a chapter on *A Midsummer Night's Dream*

Regina Buccola, *Fairies, Fractious Women and the Old Faith*, Susquehanna University Press, Selinsgrove, 2006
   A study of fairy lore in early modern drama, particularly Shakespeare's plays, including a chapter arguing for the 'Fairy Feminism' of *A Midsummer Night's Dream*

Regina Buccola, ed., *A Midsummer Night's Dream: A Critical Guide*, Continuum Renaissance Drama, Continuum, London, 2010
   Includes a critical history, a performance history and a survey of available resources, together with original critical essays

Diane Purkiss, *Troublesome Things*, Allen Lane The Penguin Press, London, 2000
   A history of fairies and their role in fiction from ancient demons to alien abduction, including Shakespeare's plays and in particular the character of the puck

Kiernan Ryan, *Shakespeare's Comedies*, Palgrave Macmillan, London, 2009
   A close reading of ten of the comedies, accessible and stimulating

LATE TWENTIETH-CENTURY CRITICS

Richard Dutton, ed., *A Midsummer Night's Dream: Contemporary Critical Essays*, New Casebooks, Macmillan, Houndmills, 1996
   A useful collection, featuring several critics noted in the **Contemporary approaches** section of **Part Five: Critical debates** – including Shirley Nelson Garner, Adrian Montrose, Elliot Krieger, Terence Hawkes and Philip C. McGuire

Helen Hackett, *A Midsummer Night's Dream*, Writers and their Work, Northcote House, Plymouth, 1997
   Several late twentieth century approaches deftly woven into a brief, accessible study

Peter Hollindale, *A Midsummer Night's Dream*, Penguin Critical Studies, London, 1992
   A thoughtful account of the play which ranges widely, yet manages to focus closely on the text

EARLIER CRITICS

Bertrand Evans, *Shakespeare's Comedies*, Clarendon Press, Oxford, 1960
   The classic study of Shakespeare's dramatic irony, featuring some helpful analysis of *A Midsummer Night's Dream*

Harold Bloom, ed., *William Shakespeare's A Midsummer Night's Dream*, Modern Critical Interpretations, Chelsea House, New York, 1987
   A collection of critics' views, including extracts from Jan Kott and Northrop Frye

Northrop Frye, *Northrop Frye on Shakespeare*, Yale University Press, New Haven and London, 1986
   A chapter devoted to the play offers a clear and concise breakdown of its elements, using literary and mythological contexts as a guide to meaning

Stephen Fender, *A Midsummer Night's Dream*, Studies in English Literature, Edward Arnold, London, 1968
   A short study with a particularly useful focus on language

Antony W. Price, ed., *Shakespeare: A Midsummer Night's Dream, A Collection of Critical Essays*, Casebooks, Macmillan, Houndmills, 1983
   A wide-ranging anthology of comments from 1607 to 1974, including G. K. Chesterton, Frank Kermode, Stephen Fender and David P. Young

David P. Young, *Something of Great Constancy*, Yale Studies in English, Yale University Press, New Haven and London, 1966
   A discussion of the play as a subtle work of art, challenging the assumption that it is a mere lightweight comedy

LITERARY TERMS

alliteration a sequence of repeated consonantal sounds, usually at the beginnings of words or stressed syllables. The sound pattern may reinforce patterns of meaning in the language. 'Following *d*arkness like a *d*ream' (V.1.364)

allusion a reference, often only indirect, to another person, event, etc.

antithesis the placing of contrasting ideas in adjacent clauses or sentences, using parallel forms of words. 'Since night you loved me; yet since night you left me' (III.2.275)

ballad a song or poem which tells a story in simple, **colloquial** language, using a traditional **verse** form

blank verse unrhymed **iambic pentameter**; the normal **metre** of Elizabethan drama. Its popularity is due to its flexibility and relative closeness to the rhythms of spoken English

characterisation how a writer creates characters so as to convey their personalities effectively, attract or repel our sympathies and integrate their behaviour into the story

colloquial everyday speech used by people in informal situations

comedy a broad **genre**; the word is most often used to describe a drama which is intended primarily to entertain the audience and which ends happily for the main characters. Most comedies do not concentrate on the fortunes of an individual, instead the interest is spread over a group of people; they tend to deal with low life and humble people, rather than with kings and nobles; their plots are usually elaborate, involve misunderstandings and deceptions, and move from the possibility of disaster towards a happy ending, often symbolised by a wedding

counterpoint combining two or more musical parts so that they are heard simultaneously. By extension, combining different things (such as the stories which make up *A Midsummer Night's Dream*) so that comparison, contrast and interaction between them create an overall effect which is more powerful than any of them would produce independently

couplet a pair of rhymed lines

dramatic irony a situation where the development of the plot allows the audience to know more about what is happening than do some of the characters

end-stopped line a line of **verse** in which the end of the line coincides with an essential grammatical pause

foreshadowing a literary technique whereby the author mentions events which are yet to be revealed in the narrative, either to increase dramatic tension, or to provide clues for the reader to attempt to guess what will happen next

genre the term for a kind or type of literature, such as **ballad**, **comedy** or **tragedy**

iambic pentameter an iamb is the commonest metrical foot in English verse, consisting of a weakly stressed syllable, followed by a strongly stressed syllable. An iambic pentameter is a line of five iambic feet: 'Four *days* / will *quick* / ly *steep* / them*selves* / in *night*' (I.1.7). Occasionally a **trochee** (a strongly stressed syllable, followed by a weakly stressed one) may be substituted for one of the iambs, particularly at the beginning of a line, either for emphasis or to prevent monotony: '*Happy* / be *The* / seus, *our* / re*nown* / èd *Duke*' (I.1.20)

imagery, image in its narrowest sense, an 'image' is a word-picture, describing some visible scene or object, like Oberon's description beginning, 'I know a bank where the wild thyme blows' (II.1.249). More commonly, 'imagery' refers to the figurative language (**metaphors** and **similes**) in a piece of literature – 'The iron tongue of midnight hath told twelve' (V.1.341) – or even all the words which appeal to the senses: 'And neigh, and bark, and grunt, and roar, and burn' (III.1.92)

lyric poetry which expresses the feelings and thoughts of an individual speaker, particularly in relation to the subject of love

metaphor a metaphor goes further than a comparison between two different things or ideas by fusing them together: one thing is described as being another thing, carrying over its associations: 'to see the sails conceive / And grow big-bellied with the wanton wind' (II.1.128–9)

metre the use of a linguistic feature which, repeated, creates a sense of pattern, distinguishing **verse** from **prose**. In English verse the commonest such pattern is stress- or accent-based metre, which consists of a regular arrangement of strong stresses in a stretch of language (see **iambic pentameter**)

parody an imitation of a work of literature or a literary style designed to ridicule the original

paradox a seemingly absurd or self-contradictory statement that is or may be true

pastoral a **genre** which originated in Greece in the third century BC, describing an imaginary world of simple, idealised rural life, in which shepherds and shepherdesses fall in love, enjoying a life of blissful ease, singing songs, playing the flute, and so on

personification a variety of figurative or **metaphorical** language in which things or ideas are treated as if they were human beings, with human attributes and feelings: 'Phoebe doth behold / Her silver visage in the watery glass' (I.1.209–10)

plot the plan of a literary work. More than the simple sequence of events, 'plot' suggests a pattern of relationships between events. More loosely, 'plot' may refer to the separate narratives within one larger story. For example, Elizabethan drama commonly features a 'main plot' and a 'subplot'. Unusually, *A Midsummer Night's Dream* contains three plots of roughly equal importance: the lovers' tribulations, the quarrel between the Fairy King and Queen, and the struggle to stage 'Pyramus and Thisbe'

prose any language which is not patterned by some kind of **metre**

quatrain a stanza of four lines

register a variety of language which is used in a particular situation: for example, the language of law or of newspaper headlines

rhetoric the art of writing and speaking effectively so as to persuade an audience. Ancient and medieval scholars classified various devices of language which might be employed to achieve particular rhetorical effects. Among these 'rhetorical figures' still commonly cited are, for example, **alliteration** and **antithesis**

romance a story dealing with adventures of chivalry and love. Such stories typically concern knightly quests, tournaments, magic, and contests with monsters for the sake of the heroine

satire literature which exhibits or examines vice and folly and directs laughter against them to make them appear ridiculous or contemptible

simile an explicit comparison in which one thing is said to be like another. Similes always contain the words 'like' or 'as': 'Swift as a shadow, short as any dream' (I.1.144)

soliloquy the convention in which a character in a play speaks directly to the audience, as if thinking aloud about their motives, feelings and decisions

sonnet a lyric poem, consisting of fourteen lines of **iambic pentameter**, rhymed and organised according to one of several intricate schemes. A book of 154 sonnets by Shakespeare was published in 1609, probably without his permission

stock character or figure a type of character who recurs in a **genre**, and may even be one of its defining features. A father determined to prevent his daughter's marriage and lovers who attempt to elope are figures found in many stories, including *A Midsummer Night's Dream* and *Romeo and Juliet*

symbol something which represents something else (often an idea or quality) either by analogy or association. Many symbols exist by convention and tradition. According to different conventions, a serpent may stand for wisdom or for evil. The latter is the case in *A Midsummer Night's Dream* II.1.9, II.2.152–5 and V.1.423. Writers also develop their own symbols, sometimes using them as a species of metaphor in which the exact subject of the metaphor is not made explicit and may be open to a variety of readings: for example, the moon in this play (see the section on **Imagery and symbolism** in **Part Four: Language**)

theme the abstract subject of a work; its central idea or ideas, which may or may not be explicit or obvious. A text may contain several themes or thematic interests

tragedy, tragic a story, usually a play, which traces the downfall of an individual, and shows in so doing both the capacities and limitations of human life

trochaic tetrameter a trochee is a metrical foot, consisting of a strongly stressed syllable, followed by a weakly stressed syllable. A trochaic tetrameter is a line of four trochaic feet, sometimes (as here) with the final syllable omitted: '*Now* the / *hung*ry / *li*on / *roars*' (V.1.349)

verse poetry, especially metrical writing

wit originally meaning 'sense', 'understanding' or 'intelligence' ('if I had wit enough to get out of this wood', III.1.124), during the seventeenth century the word came to refer specifically to that kind of poetic intelligence which combines or contrasts ideas and expressions in an unexpected and intellectually pleasing manner

TIMELINE

WORLD EVENTS	SHAKESPEARE'S LIFE	LITERARY EVENTS
		c1385 Geoffrey Chaucer, *The Knight's Tale*
1455 First printed book in Europe		
		1516 Thomas More, *Utopia*
1534 Church of England breaks with Rome	**1557** John Shakespeare marries Mary Arden	**1532** Machiavelli, *The Prince*
1558 Elizabeth I becomes Queen	**1564** William Shakespeare is born	
		1566 William Adlington's translation of Apuleius's *Golden Ass*
		1567 Golding's translation of Ovid's *Metamorphoses*
1576 First theatre in England opens at Shoreditch		
		1579 Sir Thomas North's translation of Plutarch's *Life of Theseus*
1582 Plague breaks out in London	**1582** Shakespeare marries Anne Hathaway	
	1583 A daughter, Susanna, is born	**1584** Reginald Scott, *The Discovery of Witchcraft*
	late 1580s – early 1590s Shakespeare probably writes *Henry VI*, parts I, II & III and *Richard III*	
	1585 The twins, Hamnet and Judith, are born	
1588 Spanish Armada defeated	**1592** Shakespeare acting in London	
	1592-4 Writes *The Comedy of Errors*	
	1594 *Love's Labour's Lost* written; Shakespeare writes exclusively for the Lord Chamberlain's Men	
1595-1603 Tyrone's rebellion in Ireland	**1595** Shakespeare writes *A Midsummer Night's Dream*	
1596 Francis Drake perishes on an expedition to the West Indies	**1596-8** *Henry IV*, parts 1 & 2 written	
	1598-9 Globe Theatre built at Southwark	
	1600 *A Midsummer Night's Dream* printed.	
	1600-1 *Hamlet* written	
1603 Elizabeth I dies	**1603** His company becomes the King's Men, patronised by James I, the new king	
1605 Discovery of Guy Fawkes's plot to destroy Parliament	**1605** First version of *King Lear*	**1605** Cervantes, *Don Quixote*
	1606 Shakespeare writes *Macbeth*	**1606** Ben Johnson, *Volpone*; Edward Sharpham, *The Fleire*
	1613 Globe Theatre burns down	
	1616 Shakespeare dies	
1620 The *Mayflower* takes the Pilgrim Fathers to Massachusetts	**1623** First collected volume of Shakespeare's plays published	

REVISION FOCUS TASK ANSWERS

TASK 1

It is only the presence of the fairies that makes the four lovers' quarrels entertaining.

- Hermia's pursuit of Demetrius and his attempts to escape from her are comic without any need for magic intervention.
- The puck's misapplication of the juice develops the existing conflict, setting all four lovers at odds with one another.
- Although the puck initiates the complications, it is the reactions of the lovers which complete the joke, as they give free reign to their emotions, oblivious of their origin.

The most important source of comedy in the play is dramatic irony.

- Dramatic irony is used to great effect on many occasions, such as Helena lamenting that she is 'ugly' when Lysander is about to wake up and acclaim her as beautiful.
- There are other important sources of humour in the play, such as the craftsmen's blundering efforts to perform their **tragedy**.
- There is also much verbal humour, including the craftsmen mixing up their words and the lovers descending from romantic compliments to vulgar insults.

TASK 2

Robin Goodfellow's pranks are more cruel than amusing.

- The puck undeniably terrifies the craftsmen and degrades Queen Titania.
- From the perspective of the audience, who see the events as part of a comic play, the reactions of his victims are highly amusing.
- The audience also knows that in the end Oberon will intervene to reprimand the puck.

The craftsmen are mere stereotypes whom we are expected to look down upon.

- Comedy often employs stereotypes; the lovers' overwrought emotions are just as much of a caricature as the craftsmen's ignorance and naiveté.
- Even though the craftsmen's efforts may be laughable, we are led to admire their dedication and perseverance, so much so that 'Pyramus and Thisbe' is the climax of the play.
- Bottom's initiative and resilience make him the most engaging of all the mortals.

TASK 3

The story finishes with Act IV and logically the play should end there too.

- Although Titania and Oberon have made up by the end of Act IV and the lovers' conflicts have been resolved, the craftsmen have yet to perform 'Pyramus and Thisbe'.
- Act V allows us to see all the married couples happy and at ease, imparting an emotional resolution to the play.
- The story of 'Pyramus and Thisbe' completes the play by allowing us to glimpse love's tragic aspect, counterbalancing the comedy.

The problems with which the play begins vanish without any satisfactory explanation in Act IV.

- In Act I Scene 1 Oberon says he cannot 'extenuate' Hermia's punishment, yet in Act IV he does precisely this, overruling her father Egeus.
- In Act II Scene 1 Titania vigorously defies Oberon, but in Act IV she seems passively to accept the prank played on her and the loss of her Indian boy.
- The play is not intended to be realistic, but to entertain by placing characters in far-fetched situations; once one of these has been explored, the story simply moves on.

TASK 4

There is little to choose between Lysander and Demetrius.

- Lysander is loyal and supportive to Hermia, up until the magic juice is put on his eyes.
- In contrast, Demetrius rejects Helena and seeks a forced marriage with Hermia, even though he knows that she does not love him.
- Neither character is developed in depth, as this would distract attention from the comic action.

The speeches of the lovers have often been drastically cut and rightly so.

- Shortening the lovers' scenes is probably the least damaging way to quicken the pace of the play and reduce its running time.
- The lovers' arguments become more heated and therefore more amusing the longer they go on.
- The four-way confrontation in Act III Scene 2 builds up to insults and a duel, seamlessly triggering a second comic argument straight after, when the dismayed Oberon blames the puck.

TASK 5

The play ridicules marriage, implying that magic is needed to make it work.

- Titania and Oberon quarrel fiercely, Hippolyta seems uncomfortable with Theseus, and Demetrius wants to marry Helena only because he is under a spell; the play does not show any truly happy marriages.
- The play shows that love and marriage can easily break down.
- However, the play ends with three hopeful marriages and implies, especially through the craftsmen, that fulfilment can be found by taking on new roles in life.

Beneath the comedy, the play offers a bleak view of love's irrationality.

- Lysander and Demetrius change their loves as soon as the magic juice is applied, caricaturing 'love at first sight'.
- Titania's love for Bottom is an extreme version of the same behaviour, suggesting how someone can become fixated on an entirely unsuitable partner.
- 'Pyramus and Thisbe' reminds us that love can even lead to tragic misunderstandings and suicide.

TASK 6

Written for the Elizabethan theatre, the play may seem out of place on today's stage.

- Language and theatrical conventions have changed since Shakespeare's day and a modern audience may find some features challenging, such as the large amounts of figurative language and description which have to be taken in by ear.
- Despite changes in society, the types of character (e.g. rulers, lovers and clowns) remain easy to understand and appreciate.
- The action of the drama (e.g. arguments, pranks and chases) also remains easily comprehensible.

There are no great parts for actors in *A Midsummer Night's Dream*.

- Like many comedies, the play relies on ensemble acting, each actor contributing to the whole; it does not require a 'star turn' to make it successful.
- Each part offers the actor opportunities to develop amusing character details.
- The role of Bottom does offer considerable scope for charisma and improvisation, provided the actor does not work up their part so much that it spoils the balance of the three plots.

MARK SCHEME

Use this page to assess your answer to the Worked task, provided on pages 96–7.

Aiming for an A grade? Fulfil all the criteria below and your answer should hit the mark.*

> **How far do you agree that Shakespeare portrays Bottom as an admirable character rather than a fool?**

A01 Articulate creative, informed and relevant responses to literary texts, using appropriate terminology and concepts, and coherent, accurate written expression.

- You make a range of clear, relevant points about Bottom and how he is portrayed by Shakespeare.
- You write a balanced essay covering both positions, i.e. that he can be seen as admirable but also as a fool at times.
- You use a range of literary terms correctly, e.g. **comedy**, **characterisation**, **wit**, **soliloquy**, **theme**.
- You write a clear introduction, outlining your thesis, and provide a clear conclusion.
- You signpost and link your ideas.

A02 Demonstrate detailed critical understanding in analysing the ways in which structure, form and language shape meanings in literary texts.

- You explain the techniques and methods Shakespeare uses to present the character of Bottom and link them to main themes of the text.
- You may discuss, for example, Bottom's disruptive but enthusiastic contributions to the preparation of the craftsmen's play; his response to his transformation into Titania's ass-headed lover; his full-blooded performance as Pyramus.
- You explain in detail how your examples affect meaning, e.g. Bottom's comment to Titania that 'reason and love keep little company together nowadays' (III.1.120–1) is admirably clear-sighted compared to the naïve view of love taken by other characters.
- You may explore how the setting of the stage for 'Pyramus and Thisbe' in Act V enables Bottom to go beyond lower class deference, answering back to his superiors and attempting to dazzle them with his heroic acting.

A03 Explore connections and comparisons between different literary texts, informed by interpretations of other readers.

- You make relevant links between Bottom's courtesy towards the fairies and the behaviour of the aristocrats.
- When appropriate, you compare and contrast the presentation of Bottom's positive initiatives in *A Midsummer Night's Dream* with the presentation of comic schemes in other text(s), e.g. the participation of Feste in the malicious plots in *Twelfth Night*.
- You incorporate and comment on critics' views of how Bottom is presented in the play.
- You assert your own independent view clearly.

A04 Demonstrate understanding of the significance and influence of the contexts in which literary texts are written and received.

You explain how relevant aspects of social, literary and historical contexts of *A Midsummer Night's Dream* are significant when interpreting the character of Bottom. For example, you may discuss:

- Literary context: Shakespeare's plays often feature a fool who is an uneducated clown but also a shrewd commentator.
- Historical context: Bottom's garbled reference to the Bible (IV.1) suggests there must be a deeper meaning to his words.
- Social context: the participation of weavers in contemporary riots and rebellions may add force to Bottom's outspokenness, and in this context his good nature can be seen as reassuring.

* This mark scheme gives you a broad indication of attainment, but check the specific mark scheme for your paper/task to ensure you know what to focus on.